Manual of Football
Drills and Skills

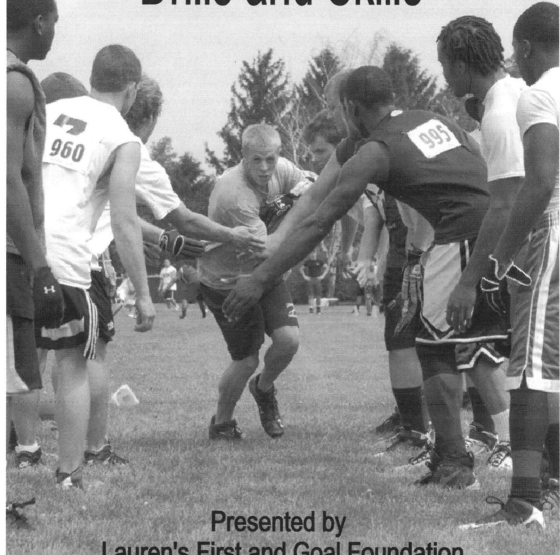

Presented by
Lauren's First and Goal Foundation

Lauren's First and Goal Foundation
and
Lauren's First and Goal Football Camps

Lauren's First and Goal Foundation is a 501(c)3 charitable organization, a labor of love started in 2004 by John and Marianne Loose in honor of their daughter, Lauren, a pediatric brain tumor survivor. The Loose family started the Foundation as a way to help other families who are battling childhood cancer.

Since its inception, LFG has raised more than $1 million toward its mission to provide financial support for brain tumor research and cancer services, to offer financial and emotional support to families living with pediatric cancer, and to increase awareness of the disease. These goals are made possible through the funding gained through LFG Football Camps and charitable contributions.

LFG Football Camps in Pennsylvania, Florida, Ohio and New York, the primary fundraisers for the Foundation, are staffed by experienced college coaches from across all divisions who volunteer their time and talent to support the mission of the Foundation. In seven years, 759 different coaches have volunteered at the camps and 9,773 high school student-athletes from 1,158 schools have attended. The camps and Foundation are operated through the generosity of volunteers.

For more information about LFG Foundation and Camps visit www.laurensfirstandgoal.org.

Board of Directors
- J. Andreassi, Director of Development, AHRC of Suffolk County, NY
- Dawn Comp, Senior Athletic Trainer/Rehabilitation Coordinator, Lafayette College
- Leo Govoni, Director and Co-Founder of the Special Needs Trust Administration
- Matt Hachmann, Assistant Football Coach, Towson University
- Charles Henry, Operations Manager (retired), Menasha Corporation
- John Loose, Lauren's father, Assistant Football Coach, Lafayette College
- Marianne Loose, Lauren's mother
- Richard Philips, Senior Vice-President, FTN Financial
- John Troxell, Head Football Coach, Franklin and Marshall College
- Pamela Troxell, Director, Lauren's First and Goal Foundation
- Daniel Weiss, President, Lafayette College

Honorary Members of Board of Directors
A special thank you to these gentlemen for their time, generosity and support of LFG.
- Randy Edsall, Head Coach, University of Maryland
- John Harbaugh, Head Coach, Baltimore Ravens
- Ken Niumatalolo, Head Coach, U.S. Naval Academy
- Jim Tressel, Head Coach, Ohio State University

Acknowledgements

The incredible success of Lauren's First and Goal Foundation would not be possible without the generous support of thousands of people across the country. What began as a close circle of family and friends making a simple attempt to help others, has quickly expanded to the multitude of kindhearted, giving members of the ever-growing Lauren's Circle of Strength.

Lauren's First and Goal Foundation would like to express its deep gratitude and thanks to those who have taken part in supporting the mission of the Foundation. Thanks to the board members, honorary board members, coaches, players, volunteers, and community fundraisers who have contributed their individual time and talents to further our mission.

We are sincerely grateful to the 137 coaches who have contributed to the first LFG Manual of Football Drills and Skills, providing a source for coaches to get the best ideas from the top in the profession. Special thanks are also extended to Ryan Hess, Lafayette College Football Operations, who contributed countless hours formatting the drill submissions, Ryan O'Neil, LFG intern and Patrice Domozych for editing the text in each drill submission.

All proceeds from the sale of this book go directly to LFG Foundation to support its mission.

For more information about LFG Foundation and Football Camps visit
www.laurensfirstandgoal.org.

Cover Page Photo by Brielle Messerschmidt

Introduction

One person can facilitate big change. Sometimes it is the smallest of people who inspire that change. Lauren Loose, a child from Easton, Pennsylvania, is the perfect example.

Lauren's incredible story motivates thousands of high school athletes and hundreds of college football coaches to converge on a Pennsylvania college campus in early June each year. It's not the hunt for recruits, the thrill of competition or the dream of being recruited by a top college football program - they come for her. She inspires both grown men and teenage boys to ponder mental toughness and the importance of family. It is Lauren's honest belief in dreams come true and hope for a better future for children with cancer, like herself, that has fueled the fire of these players, coaches and, for that matter, just about everyone who meets her.

Lauren is an inspiration and beacon of hope. It is as simple as that. She is a child with a relentless, courageous spirit and joy for life. She has the power to turn heads with her crazy laugh and infectious smile. She is happiest when she is giving or helping someone else. Lauren touches the lives of those who meet her in a profound and permanent way.

When Lauren was diagnosed with multiple brain tumors at the age of two, she and her family were faced with years of doctor visits, scans, hospitalizations and the kind of worry and uncertainty that can be debilitating. The Loose family shared these experiences with countless other families facing similar circumstances. With their hands seemingly tied by limited treatment options and gaping holes in research funding, the Looses decided to do something productive to help themselves and others.

Camp day is a real life demonstration that each of us has something positive to contribute. Whether one comes to play football, volunteer, coach or just observe, each person is part of Lauren's Circle of Strength and Hope that we want to continue to grow each year.

Thank you to our family, friends, all of the coaches, volunteers, participants and donors who help to make the Foundation and camp a success. The endless and overwhelming outpouring of support, help and prayers never ceases to amaze us and always renews our faith in the true goodness and generosity of both friends and strangers alike. We sincerely appreciate your gifts of time, talent enthusiasm and support. We are committed to making a positive difference in the lives of children battling brain tumors and pediatric cancer, and we honor your commitment to helping us to make that change.

For more information about LFG Foundation and LFG Football Camps visit
www.laurensfirstandgoal.org

Table of Contents

GAME MANAGEMENT

Photo by Michael Garner

GAME MANAGEMENT

Joe Susan, Head Coach, Bucknell University

So much time is traditionally spent…

- Evaluating your opponent
- Creating a game plan
- Planning your practice

You must plan the game!

If you do not prepare to control the game the game will control you, or your opponent will.

Will review things

- Game day preparation
- Time management
- Will impact outcome
- Detail of little things

Game day considerations

Weather conditions

- Wet   More dry balls
- Wind   Impact two quarters
- Heat   Hydration sideline
- Cold   Skill players
- Sun   Can impact the passing game

All can impact how you call the game

Opening sequence any changes or adaptations

- Advantage you might have
- What you want to see from a defense
- What you want to show
- Hold for red zone
- 2ND half openers for first possession

PERSONNEL
- Assign someone to watch pre-game
- Evaluate and time snappers
- Listen for cadence, don't use yours
- Look for starters
- Look for injuries
- Returns, how they handle the ball
- Look for obvious bracing/taping

Box field – phone checks

Field check, field markings

Quality of surface part better/worse

Position of the 25 second clock for the QB

With no 25 second clock, have a stop clock

Half-time meeting organization

Prepare half-time board

Time and script pre-game, coach it

Discuss coin toss options with captains

Over time prep – who takes the coin toss

Stay ahead of adjustments

1. Work between each series
2. Get feedback, give feedback
3. Better prepared for half-time
4. Half-time focus what you work on
5. Overhead or white board
6. Set a script of 2ND half openers
7. Any change in field options

BE TIME EFFICIENT

IMPORTANT CLOCK FACTS

1. When the field clock is the official game time, the referee is NOT required to notify captains and coaches that two minutes remain.
2. After a score, (FG, TD, Safety) the clock starts when the kickoff is legally touched in the field of play.
3. The referee will stop the clock for an injured player to be removed from the game and no time out will be charged to the team. The clock will start with the referee's signal or snap depending on how the previous play ended.
4. Referee must notify captains and coach of the number of remaining time outs they have.
5. Automatic time out by CAPTAINS/COACHES asking or discussing measurement for first down is not charged against three legal time outs. CAPTAINS/COACHES, be careful not to WASTE TIME in asking for this measurement.

GENERAL RULES OR GUIDELINES (2 MINUTES)

Everyone knows whether the clock starts with the Referee's SIGNAL or SNAP.

A. The clock starts on the "snap" in the following situations:
- After a charged time out (3 per half)
- After a change of possession (fumble, interception, punt, held-on downs or kickoff)
- After an incomplete pass
- After a penalty if time was out after the play in question
- After out of bounds play
- After touchback (field goal, punt)
- After a change of quarter

B. The clock starts on the Official's Ready For Play
- When offense is awarded a first down if ball is in bounds
- After a referee's timeout for an injured player or official if time was in
- At the referee's discretion
- After a penalty if time was in after the play in question
- For an inadvertent whistle (except free kick)
- For a head coach's conference
- For a sideline warning
- For an illegal pass to conserve time

TIME OUT CONSERVATION

A. Do not call timeout when the clock is stopped unless instructed to do so.
B. Do not call timeout when you have a second play called unless you feel that too much time will be lost in getting the second play off.
C. Do not call timeout with more than one minute remaining unless you have all three timeouts left.
D. Do not call a timeout with more than one minute remaining unless you have all three timeouts left, the clock is running, and you do not have a second play called
   - maybe you have audibles in the game plan for this situation.
E. Consider calling a timeout prior to any 4th down play.
F. Call timeout in the final 60 seconds when you have all 3 timeouts left and the clock is running.
G. Call timeout in the final 60 seconds when you have ONE timeout left, the clock is running and you do not have a second play called. (Maybe you have audibles in the game plan for this situation. Will conserve time out)
H. Try to save a timeout to get the field-goal team into the game.

Essentials to Consider

1. Fast field goal – practice it
2. Ability to "center" the ball and stop the clock
3. Time left for last field goal
3RD DOWN	9 sec
4TH DOWN	3 sec
4. Variations of the "Last Play of the Game"

Know what you need

Do you have time to run deep outs?

Does it have to be traditional?

A play to keep the ball in play

How to practice:
Preparation ready to defend
Four Minute Offense

1. Do not call timeout.
2. Use full 25 seconds on each play.
3. Keep runners away from the sideline.
4. Runners and receivers stay in bounds.
5. Protect the ball with two hands and get up slowly.
6. Avoid penalties.
7. Stay in the huddle with less than 25 seconds remaining.
8. Ultimately use "VICTORY" formation.

STRENGTH & CONDITIONING

4th QUARTER WINS

Brad Potts, Director of Performance Enhancement, Lafayette College

Let me start out by saying that it is without question, in the field of Performance Enhancement (Strength and Conditioning), well thought out plans backed by scientific research that have proven effective through real world application usually works best when trying to get our athletes in optimal playing shape. That being said, there are times we need to forget about the science and just see what our team is made of!!!

At Lafayette College we want our athletes to be comfortable and calm in stressful situations, thus proficiently processing information. That is our reasoning behind our 4th quarter win session, we are not talking bioenergetics….we are talking about pushing your mind, with the confidence that your body will follow!!

The following instructions describe the flow our 2011 four quarter win sessions. The session starts on 4th Saturday of our eight week off-season phase which is a de-loading week. This is done **in hopes** of making the first session as safe and successful as possible.

Please see the Diagram when reading:

- Divide the team up into groups of 6. Place one man on each end of The Strongman Competitions. Three guys on the start side compete across the field and the three guys on the other side bring it back. Whoever wins is out of the 1st gauntlet station (grass drills) that they immediately proceed to.
- The athletes then proceed directly to the gauntlet where the remaining four who did not win the strongman participate in 2 man competitive grass drills. Whoever wins the grass drill is out of the next station. This will progress the rest of the gauntlet. You will NEVER have more than four people in a drill in the whole gauntlet.
- Then onto the King of the Ring. This is where the coaches place the players of their choice together to see who is willing to fight when they are completely exhausted. Sometimes if the coach is not satisfied with the efforts, the athletes will wrestle several times until the loser gets the point.
- Then we pin the winners of The King of the Ring against the losers in our next station The Tug of War.
- The **winners** of the tug of war carry their teammate 100 yards on their backs to the finish line.
- Repeat until desired results are achieved!!

> If you have any questions contact me or come up and watch a workout.
> God Bless,
> Brad Potts M.S. CSCS USAW
> Director of Performance Enhancement
> Lafayette College
> Pottsb@lafayette.edu (610) 330-5526

4th QUARTER WINS

Brad Potts, Director of Performance Enhancement, Lafayette College

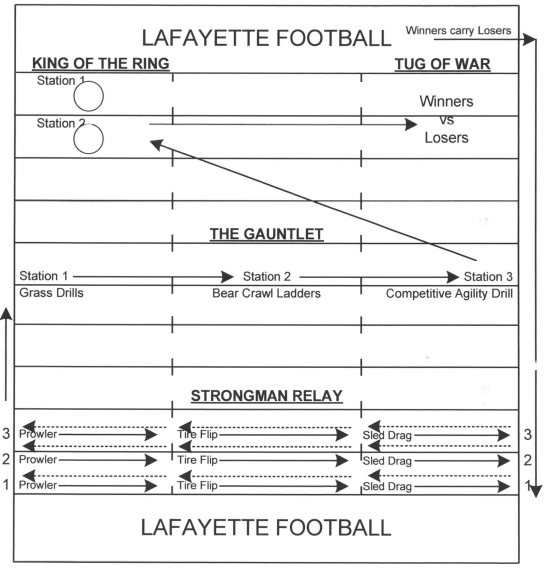

AMC SUMMER RUNNING
Marc Klaiman, Head Coach, Anna Maria College

4 CONE DRILL

4 Cones set in a 10 yard by 10 yard square.

A. Cut to your Left – Come Under Control, Plant on your Right foot and Cut to your Left.
B. Cut to your Left – Come Under Control, Plant on your Right foot and Cut to your Left.
C. Sprint – Shuffle – Back Pedal – Shuffle
D. Sprint – Carioca – Back Pedal – Carioca
E. Sprint – Pass Drop @ 45 – Sprint – Pass Drop @ 45 (Figure 2)
F. Back Pedal – Forward Break @ 45 – Back Pedal – Forward Break @ 45 (Figure 2)

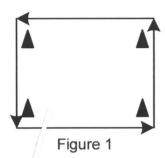

Figure 1

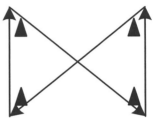

Figure 2

NEBRASKA

Run a Figure 8 around Cone 2
Sprint back to Cone 1
Back Pedal to Cone 2
Sprint to Cone 1

AMCAT

Sprint to Cone 2
Shuffle from Cone 2 to Cone 1
Sprint to Cone 2
Shuffle (opposite way) from Cone 2 to Cone 1
Back Pedal to Cone 2
Sprint to Cone 1

OFFENSE

Photo by Brielle Messerschmidt

NOTES

OFFENSIVE LINE

Photo by Michael Garner

OL LEVERAGE DRILLS
Ron Crook, Stanford University, Offensive Line

LEVERAGE DRILLS:

I believe that leverage drills are the most important drills you can have your
players do as an O-line coach. We all try to get perfect footwork and targets on every block.
However, for a number of reasons, this does not always happen. Leverage drills allow your
players to drive their feet and knees through the defender to get movement, even if we are not in
perfect position.

LEVERAGE DRILL:

We start in a fit position. The defender should be in a low position applying pressure into the
blocker. On the cadence, we drive our back side foot / knee through the defender. As we run our
feet, we try to drive our knees into the defender every step. The defender should drive toward the
blocker's face (like a D-Linemen would if he was getting blocked).

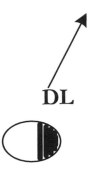

2-ON-1 LEVERAGE:

This is done with two defenders and one blocker. Start in fit position with one shoulder / hand on
each defender. The drill is the same as above, but we are now trying to drive both defenders
down the field. Again, the defenders should make it difficult to drive them, but since it is an
offensive drill, they should let the blocker win the drill.

BLOCKING THE GUN-TRIPLE OPTION

Ralph Isernia, Offensive Coordinator, University of Charleston

This set of drills will be done on the one-man sled. We use this to emphasize balance and base. The sled will be set on a yard line working across the field to ensure players are working in a straight line. A coach will stand next to the lineman holding a stick over his head to ensure he stays low out of his stance. We can also use the one-step, two-step progression if the technique is not perfect. These are all done from a good stance, right foot then left foot lead and done two times or to coach's satisfaction.

1. Drive – Square up to the sled, 8 inch vertical power step, roll the back knee for leverage

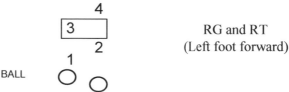

RG and RT
(Left foot forward)

2. Veer – Off-set on sled so veer foot is centered on bag, 8 inch step on 45 degree angle, roll the back knee for leverage

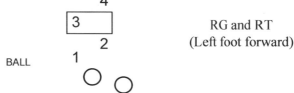

RG and RT
(Left foot forward)

3. Doubles – Blast – Double team blocks, driving the sled, matching steps, Post man and Rip man, stay on the block

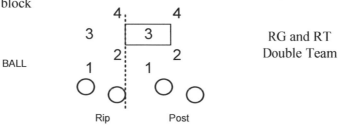

RG and RT
Double Team

A. Post technique – Veer steps, good arm sweep, make contact on second step, inside hand on sternum, outside hand through near number, accelerate feet on contact.
B. Rip technique – Drive steps, good arm sweep, make contact on second step, rip forearm up under shoulder pads and through near number, keep inside arm free by pumping it, accelerate feet on contact.

4. Doubles – Reads – Same double drill but incorporate a LB to read and block

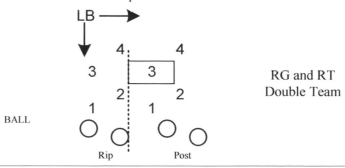

RG and RT
Double Team

"BOOFS"

John Strollo, Offensive Line Coach, Ball State University

In these drills, "B" clamps the "BOOF" ball against his chest by folding his arms over the top of the ball. He must have his mass and weight to the ball. Prayer Hands... Low strike [Rhino, Bear] point fingers at opponent's feet... High strike [Cobra] point fingers at opponent's numbers.

2 Step Rhino - Strike from the same platform. Partners, face each other. A assumes the big tree. He has great posture. His feet are in a position "on same platform" as B, so that he can land a lifting strike. He forms the "horn", his elbows are low, his hands are lower than his elbows. Prayer hands are low.

"A" will land six pulling strikes. He is violent, not frantic. He will make this "BOOF" sound on each strike. The emphasis is on the upper arm lift and tight hands. His hands must go from "closed book" to "open book" and his arms form horn to pull B out of the ground. After each strike, take 2 steps forward. Alternate right and left. Each "2 step" puts you back into the "Big Tree". A and B exchange rolls. Repeat the drill twice.

2 Step Bear – Partners, face each other. A is braced in a right stagger and looks right. One foot on the platform, one in the block. Feet are at 90 degree vector... He forms the "Horn", his elbows are low, his hands are low, his hands are lower than his elbows. Prayer hands are low.

"A" will land three pinning strikes. He is violent, not frantic. He will make the "BOOF" sound on each strike. The emphasis is on upper arm lift and tight hands. His hands must go from "Meatball" to "Bucket" and his arms form hooks to pin B to the wall. After each strike, he will "Anchor Brace" while maintaining the braced stagger position. On the "release" command, A will snap B, trying to throw the ball. A and B exchange roles with B driving A back to the origin. They repeat the drill.

Shuffle R/L – Strike timing the "Boof" from a shuffle and pull man out of the ground. "A" is in the stance of the day at the bottom left corner of a square, "B" is in the top right, facing "A" and holding a medicine ball.

From the stance, "A" will shuffle right while "B" mirrors. At the far side of the square, "A" will gallop forward as "B" attacks. "A" will shuffle, strike and pull "B" out of the ground. "A" will not arrow. **Stay square to LOS. When moving right, maintain the braced stagger until contact. Land "Rhino" strike.** On the "release" command, "A" and "B" exchange roles with "B" driving "A" back to the origin. They repeat drill in the respective other direction.

In these drills, "B" clamps the "Boof" ball against his chest by holding the ball on his chest. He must add his mass to the ball and brace against the strike.

Cobra 3 Right, 3 Left – Strike time the snap and brace from a stagger. "A" opposes "B" at more than arm's length. "A" is in a stagger, pass set demeanor. "B" holds the medicine ball in his hands against his chest.

"B" will attack "A", who in turn will snap the ball. Prior to contact the brace foot is in the air. On contact, "A" will brace to a block. "B" will rebound away and attack "A" two more times. Emphasis is on short violent snap, posture and strike timing. Prayer hands are high, open hood of cobra to strike. "A" and "B" exchange roles and repeat. Then they repeat the drill in the opposite stagger.

TEACHING THE DOUBLE TEAM COMBO BLOCK

Tim Kepple, Offensive Line Coach, Salve Regina University

This technique is taught to offensive linemen when we want to keep them square on the double team before getting off to the next level. This is not the type of double team combo blocks we use on our outside zone plays, which is a whole separate teaching progression.

Teaching the Double Team:
The biggest problem with most double team blocks is getting split by the defensive lineman. We emphasize getting, and keeping, the hips together. Additionally, I put a high priority on keeping the man side leg up.

Progression:
- Gallop
- Gallop with resistance
- Hip slam with shield and gallop
- Hip slam with shield and gallop adding a defender for resistance

Gallop:
This is something I began to learn about around 3 years ago and started teaching 2 years ago. I believe this new technique has solidified moving the defender off the line of scrimmage. The best way for me to describe this technique is to think of the knights from Monty Python on their imaginary horses galloping through the forest (only with a flatter back). One leg is up and that is the strong leg (man side leg is up). The back leg is for pushing, you are not going to go really fast with this technique but you will have more power. Each lineman will learn to gallop with either leg forward and either leg as the push off leg. Once the players have learned the basic movement, we move on to the next step.

Gallop with resistance:
The next step in the progression is learning to gallop with some resistance. At first, I use a player holding a shield. He will give the two linemen working somewhat in conjunction a little resistance. For this part of the progression I am mainly interested in getting movement with a proper galloping gait.

Hip Slam with a shield and gallop:
We start the next progression on air. I stand behind the linemen and on my command they move their feet so that the hips come together. As they start to move I place a shield between their hips. They squeeze their hips together and with the shield leg up, they must hold the shield between their hips and gallop for five yards.

Hip Slam with a shield and gallop adding a defender for resistance:
The final part of this progression is to add a defender. We first have the defender use a shield for light resistance. As the offensive linemen become more proficient at the drill, the defender will give greater resistance up to the point of live contact. We still insist on keeping the shield held between the hips.

UTICA OFFENSIVE LINE DRILLS

George Penree, Offensive Line Coach, Utica College

Base Block Drill:

Purpose: Teach offensive linemen proper leverage, hand placement, drive, and finish on inside running plays.

Setup: You will need two offensive linemen and two yard lines. One OL is on the starting line and the other is facing him, lined up on defense. The defensive linemen is either lined up head up, inside shade, or outside shade.

Execution: The offensive player can be in a fit position the first rep. On coach's command he will execute a base block and finish for five yards. He wants to be in the leverage position on the first step and climb the block on the second. He wants to maintain heavy feet for five yards not allowing his feet to get too far ahead of each other. After five yards the player on the defense will come back executing a base block on coach's command.

Variation: The offensive lineman and defensive lineman can be in a stance. This will teach the block from start to finish.

Reach Block Drill:

Purpose: Teach your offensive lineman proper leverage, hand placement, drive, and finish on outside running plays.

Setup: You will need 2 offensive lineman and 2 yard lines. One offensive lineman is on the offense on a yard line, the other is on defense facing him. Set him either head up/left shade/right shade.

Execution: This is a 3 step command drill. The first step is the depth and width step to gain head and hip position. The second step is the crossover step to gain the reach position (contact is made on the second step). The third step is the run step to finish the block. On the first whistle the offensive lineman takes his depth and width step. The second whistle the offensive lineman makes contact with INSIDE HAND. Third whistle they will continue to run their feet and finish the block for 5 yards.

Down Block Drill:

Purpose: Teach offensive linemen proper leverage, hand placement, drive, and finish on plays requiring down or seal blocks.

Setup: You will need two offensive lineman and two yard lines. One offensive lineman is on the offense while the other is on defense facing him. Set him either head up/left shade/right shade.

Execution: The offensive player can be in a stance. This is a 3 step command drill. On the first whistle the offensive player steps to the V of the neck of the defender. On the second whistle he will put his helmet in the armpit of the defender. On the third whistle he will finish the block for 5 yards. On coach's command he will execute a down block and finish for five yards.

Variation: Have defender come over the top on the second whistle. We counter this with a double step, meaning we settle step as he comes over the top and power shuffle to gain position.

OFFENSIVE LINE PASS GAME FUNDAMENTALS & DRILL DESCRIPTIONS

Ed Warinner, Offensive Line Coach, University of Notre Dame

Mirror:

Set two cones on the sideline of the field on the inside of a line 5 yards apart. Have a partner across from you be the designated runner (rabbit) and have him give you a cadence to start the set from a 2 or 3 point stance. Then he will run side to side, staying inside the 2 cones. You will be in your perfect set position and you will attempt to move side to side in that position maintaining half-man leverage with the rabbit. Use his ear as a visual landmark and keep your nose on his inside ear. Work the drill for 4-5 seconds, starting with both hands behind you in the small of your back. Progress to two hands up and also go one hand up. One hand up forces you to keep yourself square to the defender. Always stay inside leverage when you work the one and two hand up position.

Mirror Spin:

Have the defender lean his body into your hands with you in the perfect set alignment and posture. The defender will work side to side but will also gain ground to the imaginary QB behind you. You will always give ground and control the rabbit as he weaves you backwards. At some point during the drill, the rabbit may spin to escape your control; especially if he feels you have overplayed him to a particular edge. You may also do mirror spin with only one hand up and the other behind your back. Again the focus is on staying square. When the defender spins, execute the hand replacement fundamentals listed next.

Hand Replacement:

Partner up with the designated defensive player leaning his chest into your two hands. You are aligned in the ideal set posture. The defender will attempt to swipe your hands off his chest using a lateral, upward and downward motion. The offensive player must stay in the perfect set and replace his hands on the chest of the defender as fast as possible using a quick and small circular motion (small, quick circles work the best).

Pass Sets:

Partner up and have the designated defensive player work a 3-4 step rush up field working through the offensive player's inside or outside shoulder. The offensive player goes from a 2 or 3 point stance to a set position. Deliver a perfect punch and then move to a position for a second punch but end the drill before the second punch.

Push and Pull:

Partner up with the designated defender. Get in the set position and have the defender lean into your hands. The defender will then grab your shoulder pads and on the start signal will attempt to bull rush you. When he gets you leaning he will attempt to pull you forward. Battle the pressure by moving your feet and maintaining your stagger.

Rapid Fire – Punch Drill:

Line up four defenders in a single file line. Have the first guy in line be 2 yards from the offensive blocker and each guy behind him in line about a yard from him. They will start running at the offensive lineman when he pass sets from a stance. Each defender runs at a shoulder making sure they rotate which shoulder they attack in an alternating fashion. The second defender will not leave until the punch is completed.

ILLINOIS RUN BLOCKING DRILLS

Joe Gilbert, Assistant Head Coach / Offensive Line, University of Illinois

Run Punch (Load of Elbows)

Purpose:
Teach OL the proper punch and blow delivery. Emphasis on punch, placement and action.

Coaching Points:
- Proper stance on ground. (On knees, hips off the heels)
- Flat back
- Down hand up on tri-pod of all five fingers
- Off hand on the side of the knee
- Pull arms at shoulder back in a pendulum motion
- Hands no farther than hip with thumbs up
- Elbows next to your rib cage
- Strike with thumbs up and elbows tight
- Eyes on contact point
- Roll hips on the third punch extend arms with eyes on target

Drill:
- 5 OL will line up
- Defenders will hold bags
- On command the OL will execute 2 punches
- On 3rd punch OL will roll hips and extend through to the ground
- Finish with eyes up on land mark

Double Under Punch (Load of Elbows)

Purpose:
Teach OL the proper punch and blow delivery. Emphasis on punch, placement and action.

Coaching Points:
- Proper stance
- Weight on insteps of feet
- Toes out at ten and two o'clock
- Knees in slightly
- Slight bend in the waist and good knee bend
- Pull arms at shoulder back in a pendulum motion
- Palms are facing up with thumbs out
- Elbows next to your rib cage
- Strike with thumbs up and elbows tight
- Eyes on contact point
- Slight roll of hips with each punch
- On fifth punch duck walk and drive with fast feet
- Hold tennis ball in hands as you strike to keep
  elbows in

ILLINOIS RUN BLOCKING DRILLS

Joe Gilbert, Assistant Head Coach / Offensive Line, University of Illinois

Chutes and Boards:

Purpose:
Teach OL the proper fit and drive on a defender. You work pad level and base as you drive defender.

Coaching Points:
- Proper stance
- Work proper power angles in ankles, knees and hips
- Work steps to a contact position
- Weight on insteps of feet with toes out at 10 and 2 o'clock
- Arms in a proper fit with elbows in and thumbs out
- Short power steps forcing feet in the ground
- Eyes up as you move on target
- Continue to keep weight in the center of body
- Drive defender through the end of the chute with leverage and wide base

Drill:
- We will fill every chute
- Each OL will execute footwork, punch and drive
- Emphasis on leverage and finish

LB – Rip up to 2nd level

Purpose:
Teach OL the proper angle and leverage on a LB at the 2nd level. You must work every type of play from a toss, iso or power play.

Coaching Points:
- Proper stance
- Work proper angle to second level
- Dip – strike – drive
- Never turn unless at same level as LB
- Block him based on helmet position
- Helmet inside of you block play side number
- Helmet in front of you take near target and block at the angle you find him

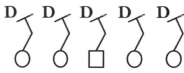

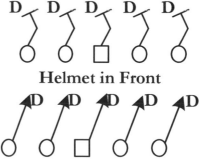

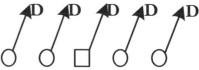

Drill:
- 5 OL will line up with LBs aligned over top of them or shade to one side
- We will work in a specific direction
- OL will work up and adjust based on LB over top or underneath

Drill adjustments:
- Can use hurdles to force offensive lineman to regain leverage
- Can use boards to keep a wide base

COMBO BLOCK DRILLS
Charles Eger, Offensive Coordinator, Widener University

Objectives:
Improve the exchange of double team of B gap defender or truck blocks
for power.

Procedure:
1. Take 6" step with inside foot keeping your head to inside shoulder of 3 technique.
2. 2nd step split the crotch of 3 technique while outside hand punches inside number of
   defender. It is very important to keep the inside arm free and off the block.
3. Drive the 3 technique back as if you were pushing a car and keep eyes to appropriate LB.
4. Once the Tackle has taken over the block double off to appropriate LB.

Tackle or TE (Truck):
1. Step with inside foot at a 45 degree angle trying to get your nose in the midline of defender.
2. Second step is in direction of defenders hip as inside hand goes to V of the neck and outside
   hand punches outside breast plate of defender.
3. Third step is through the crotch of defender and drive like pushing a car. As you drive you
   are trying to pull the 3 technique to your outside shoulder and bump of the guard with
   your butt.

Coaching Points:
Push the double 1st by driving him into the lap of LB.

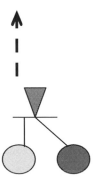
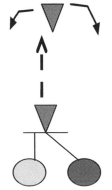

COMBO BLOCK DRILLS
Charles Eger, Offensive Coordinator, Widener University

Objectives:
To enhance the exchange of the double team between C & G for all iso doubles.

Procedures:
G & C Double on shade to LB (ISO)

Guard:
1. Guard needs to take 2 foot split to ensure a proper angle to LB.
2. Take 6" step with inside foot keeping outside arm free and head outside defenders body.
3. Drive the A gap player vertical with eyes on LB. Inside hand should be on defenders outside number.

Center:
1. Center 6" step with play side foot to crotch of defender. Push A gap player vertical and try pulling him across face.
2. It is very important the center step as he snaps to ensure that he will get his head on the play side of the defender and keeps his eyes on the appropriate LB at all times.

Coaching Points:
- Push the double 1st by driving him into the lap of LB
- Vs 1 tech C needs to get to G's hip 1st

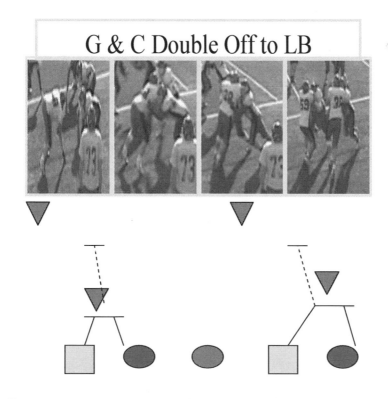

G & C Double Off to LB

OFFENSIVE LINEMAN DRILL: 3 MAN REACTION

Frank Sheehan, Offensive Line Coach, Brown University

Objective:

To teach an offensive lineman how to quickly and efficiently identify a TWIST game and block it accordingly both in the run game and pass game.

Equipment:

Cones and hand shields

Procedure:

Align 3 defensive players shoulder width apart with toes on a line holding shields against chest. Set offensive lineman on the middle defender with desired alignment in either a 3 point or 2 point stance. Command the twist you desire by directing loop and penetrator.

Coaching Points:

- It all starts with a great pass set, don't play the drill.
- Teach pre snap tips (e.g. tilts, weight distribution, cheat in stagger, alignments etc.).
- Trap the penetrator with your eyes and your feet.
- Force the loop wide by drive blocking the penetrator (1st).
- This is a great drill for OC and OG's.
- For OT's remove one of the defenders to work T/E and E/T stunts, coach the vertical set vs. with 3T inside.
- Hang on the penetrator and LATE on the loop!!!! For all tandem twist work.

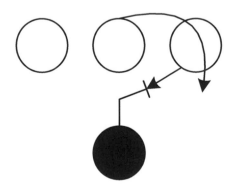

LOOP DRILL

Bill Roos, Offensive Line Coach, Marist College

Objective:

Teaching offensive linemen to pass off the looper in twists and stunts.

Equipment:

2 hand shields which represent my adjacent lineman.

Drill Format:

Establish a LOS and align the offensive lineman. Place hand shield on both sides of the lineman (only to the inside of an OT), which represents his partner. Align 3 defenders, one over the offensive lineman and on to each side. This could coincide with the front you are seeing that week. Have a coach/extra player stand behind the offensive lineman to give loop direction and then make a cadence call (2-4 groups working at one time).

Drill Progression:

On the snap of the ball the offensive lineman takes his normal pass set. When he reads the loop he yells "BUMP" to his partner. Attacks the penetrator and forces his partner onto the looping defender.

UNCOVERED

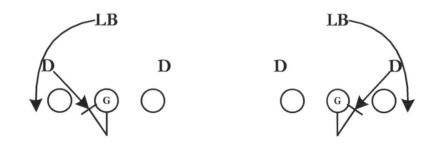

COVERED

ACCELERATION DRILL

John Reagan, Offensive Coordinator, Rice University

Purpose:

Stimulate different looks on any combination block. Promote O-Lineman understanding one hand and two hand blocking concept.

Coaching Points:

1. Only work 1/2 of the defender if covered
2. Work hips in the same direction
3. Eyes quickly move from first level to second level (feel the first level, see the second level)
4. Stay on first level until all color disappears

Equipment:

None

Description:

Align two OL with appropriate splits. Begin only with a down defensive lineman. On command, appropriate lineman takes appropriate steps (2) to moment of contact. On second command, covered lineman begins to drive through ½ man and uncovered lineman takes his steps to accelerate through the block. Begin with a static defender. Progress to a moving defender. As long as there is "color" on near shoulder of covered lineman, uncovered lineman stays on track through defender. Accelerate through the block.

Example: Zone Right

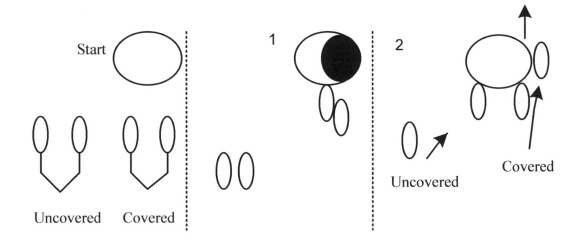

Notes:

1. Work ½ speed to full speed
2. Can use for zone blocks, double team, combination blocks
3. Only add 2nd level player after full speed with just 1 level player

LEVERAGE DRILL

John Reagan, Offensive Coordinator, Rice University

Purpose:
Force players to <u>fight</u> for proper leverage with both hands and pad level.

Coaching Points:
1. Hands inside
2. Eyes below hands
3. Power demeanor position
4. Wide base

Equipment:
Long boards

Description:
2 players with player A in fit position and player B defending. Player A has hands inside and in great position. On 1st whistle, player A drives player B down board. On 2nd whistle, player B drops pad level and fights hands inside. He then drives player A down board. Players continue to alternate on each whistle. Drill should continue for 12-15 seconds.

Example:

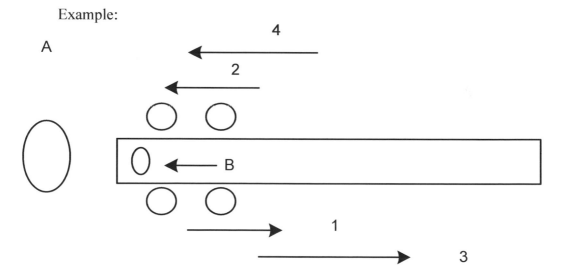

Notes:
Can be used as a conditioning drill

NAVY: INSIDE ZONE DRILL

Ashley Ingram, Offensive Line Coach, US Naval Academy
Mike Judge, Fullbacks Coach, US Naval Academy

Inside Drill

Purpose: FB and OL recognize and execute inside zone vs. various looks.

Coaching Points:
FB – Aiming point PSG, read 1st DL front side, finish through LB level.

Drill Set-up:

PSG – Uncovered: Zone, Covered: Base.
C – Scoop / Zone, secure PS A-Gap to LB. Make 1 step decision.
BSG – Scoop / Zone, secure BS A-Gap. Make 1 step decision.

Personnel:

Offense: 3 OL, 1 QB, 1 RB.
Defense: 1 or 2 DL, 1 or 2 LBs.

Drill Execution:

Coach directs defensive players according to schemes / stunts / line slants etc...

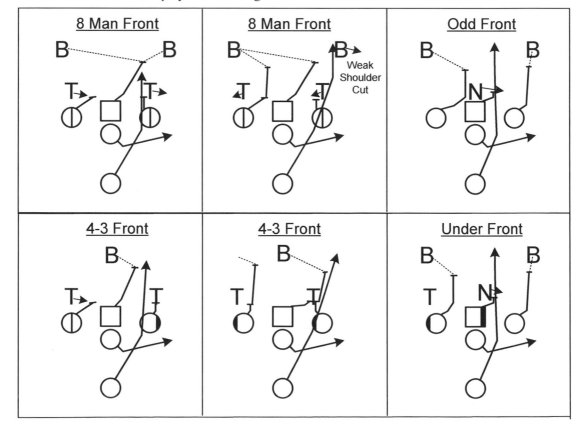

DRILLING THE TARGET & JAM

Fred Mariani, Director of Player Development, Rutgers University

Target Wave:

Procedure:

Players will pair off with each other, our 1st offensive line turns and faces the 2nd offensive line. Each pair will work in a 5x5 square area. One player acts as the coach and directs his partner. The player/coach will hold up one finger and move it both to right and left. The pass blocker will respond to the finger (target) and mirror its movement. We want the blocker to focus in on the finger tip, not the big picture. We also ask the player/coach to add kind of head weaves into the drill while keeping the finger still to make sure the pass blocker does not lose focus of the target. We then switch the players and change roles. Each player will go three times as a blocker. Remain in demeanor position as you are working the target.

Note: To improve target location and training the eyes, you can spray paint targets on practice jerseys and blocking shields. Your linemen can then focus on those objects.

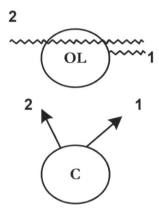

Down the Line:

Procedure:

In this drill we are isolating on the proper jam and the timing of the jam. We have one blocker lined up vs. 3 defenders. On the snap count the blocker will set and squat and slide over to the 1st defender. When the blocker is head on the defender, the defender will pass rush and attack the blocker. The blocker will be in his demeanor position and will take on the rusher with a solid 6 inch jam. After the jam, the blocker resets and slides over to the next defender and repeats the action, and then moves onto the third. We are not in a rush to move from one defender to the next. We want to concentrate on timing the jam and using a proper punch. The defender may change up the type of pass rush (swim, rip, etc.) or even fake a rush and then not follow through with it.

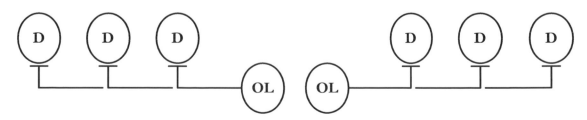

UNIVERSITY OF DELAWARE PULL DRILL

Damian Wroblewski, Assistant Head Coach, University of Delaware

Offensive Linemen align on the intersections. Defenders align based on specific pull. Each Box is 5 yards by 5 yards. Move lines based on field condition.

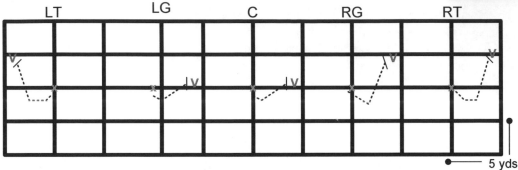

5 yds

Drills:

Directions:
Each side of the line will go separately and the center will rotate directions.

Power Pull: G'S
Footwork: Skip / Brace Down Hill
Strike: Shoulder – Pull Rt, Rt Shoulder, Pull Lt, Lt Shoulder
Finish: Strike & Accelerate through the defender with proper shoulder
Defender Align: 4X4 in Direction of Pull
Tempo: Short Block
*Centers are drilling trap block opposite direction of pulls

Wrap Pull: T's
Footwork: Drop, Cross, Drop
Strike: Shoulder – Trap Rt, Rt Shoulder, Trap Lt, Lt Shoulder
Finish: Strike & Accelerate through the defender with proper shoulder
Defender Align: 4X4 in Direction of Pull
Tempo: Short Block

Trap Pull:
Footwork: Lateral open toe step gaining ground toward the defender, gain ground up field, gain ground up field
Punch: Shoulder Strike – Trap Rt, Rt Shoulder, Trap Lt, Lt Shoulder
Finish: Strike & Accelerate through the defender with proper shoulder; Keep Head in the "Hole"
Defender Align: 3 to 4 yds. from OL; Inside foot on line
Tempo: Short Block

Outside Man Fold:
Footwork: Skip / Brace / Run
Strike: 2 Hand / Head Butt; Head on outside number
Finish: Strike & Accelerate through the defender; Get face mask off of defender
** 2 reps
1st Rep: Defender Align "Hard Defender" On LOS – 4 yards away
2nd Rep: Defender Align "Soft Defender" 4x4 in Direction of Pull
Tempo: LONG Block

Note: Plan Ahead & Think First so that players do not run into each other

3 ON 1 PUNCH – PASS PRO

Michael Clark, Head Coach, Lycoming College

Thanks to LFG for the opportunity to share a drill with other coaches. We think that this is a simple yet effective way to drill pass pro fundamentals.

The purpose of this drill is to work on footwork and punch timing for pass protectors. To get plenty of reps, we usually do this with 3 or 4 groups at a time.

Start with three defenders equally spaced in a five yard area. The offensive player will start nose to nose with the middle defender about 1 yard away. On the coach's command, the OL will kick-slide at a 45 degree angle while the outside defender rushes up field to simulate a pass rush. The OL must stop the rush of the DL with his punch. The DL will stop his rush once he is punched.

Once the first defender is punched, the 2nd defender begins his rush straight up field - not at an angle toward the OL. This will force the OL to work more (move his feet) to get to the defender. The OL should now use Post Slide Footwork to move toward the 2nd rusher. He should use his punch to stop the rush of the second DL just like he did the first.

The 3rd DL will begin his rush after the punch of the second rusher. The OL will Kick Slide back to the middle to stop the final rusher.

This is a great drill to teach footwork and timing. When the OL is finished punching all three rushers, the group rotates clockwise. As they rotate the next group can begin the same drill. This will allow one coach to see everyone doing the drill.

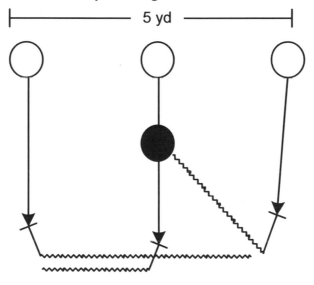

STRIKE ON THE RUN

Brian White, Offensive Line Coach, Rose-Hulman Institute of Technology

Purpose:
This drill is done early in practice to ensure that Offensive Linemen have been properly warmed-up. It also provides an opportunity to teach Offensive Linemen how to come to balance and strike a defender at the 2nd Level.

Equipment:
5 Agile Bags, 1 Shield (extra shields needed for next holders in line).

Drill:
Each Offensive Lineman runs over the Agile Bags, placing one foot in each hole. Once the Offensive Lineman reaches the end of the bag, he will come to balance with a good base and strike a rising blow on the shield. He will drive to the whistle. Look for the OL's eyes to go to the target. Also look for tight elbows on the punch and feet running through contact. Offense goes to the back of the Defensive line and vice versa.

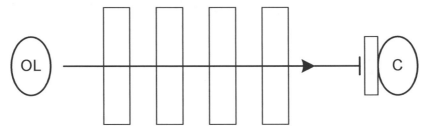

Variation:
The 2nd time through the line the shield holder is allowed to make one move (and only one move) to the left or right. This forces the Offensive Linemen to adjust his course and square the bag up. Make sure that each OL squares up to the shield. Do not let them hit from the side.

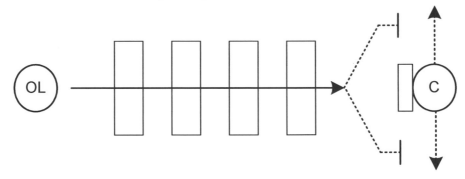

OFFENSIVE LINE DRILL

Stan Clayton, Offensive Line Coach, Lafayette College

Fit - Finish

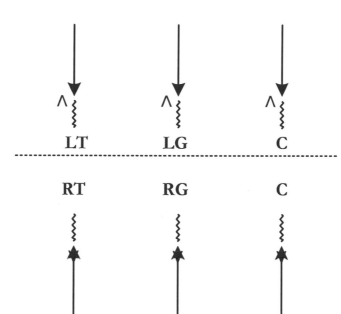

Coaching Points:

2 POINT STANCE
1. Knees bent and inside ankles.
2. Back arched. Weight balanced.
3. Feet slightly wider than shoulder width.
4. Work off of insteps.
5. Toes pointed slightly to outside.

FIT
1. Eyes lower than defenders; get a bite.
2. Punch and grab under pectoral pads.
3. Lift- snap hips on movement.

FINISH
1. Chase him with feet; accelerate.
2. Maintain base.
3. Play through to whistle.

NOTES

TIGHT ENDS

Photo by Michael Garner

TIGHT END BLOCKING DRILLS

Kevin Eick, Tight Ends Coach, Utica College

Basic Release Drills:

<u>**Purpose:**</u>
Work on technique of releases and alignment of defender.

<u>**Set-up:**</u>
Bag, Two or more guys.

<u>**Execution:**</u>
1. Line up facing a bag or stand-up.
2. Have the bag represent different possible shades.
3. Practice all methods of releases.
4. Block or Cut away from defender.
5. Catch a ball at end of drill.

<u>**Variations:**</u>
- Call out certain plays and see how player responds.
- Have bag holder shoot different gaps or drop into coverage.
- Can also use for 2nd level releases. Place defender 5 yards off ball.

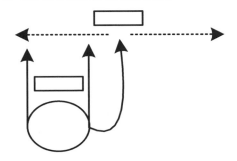

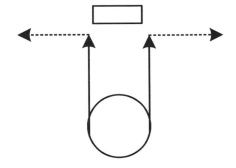

LB in Space Drill:

<u>**Purpose:**</u>
Run blocking LB in space, working a release.

<u>**Set-up:**</u>
Two Bags, Two or more guys.

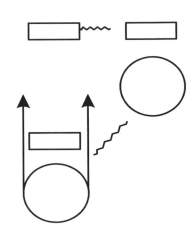

<u>**Execution:**</u>
1. Line up facing a bag with different shades.
2. Practice all methods of releases.
3. Once released, use following techniques:
   1. **Sprint**– to close distance.
   2. **Sink** – to gain leverage.
   3. **Power Shuffle** – until you reach defender.
   4. **Shoot hands** – keep elbows in, thumbs up.
   5. **Finish** – by rolling hips through defender.

<u>**Variations:**</u>
- Have bag holder shoot different gaps or drop into coverage.
- Allow for free release or other releases.

REACH RIP
Isaac Collins, Head Coach, Widener University

Objectives:
- To effectively obtain out side leverage on a zone block.

Reach Step:
- To reach a wide technique first step is a bucket w/ outside foot (wider the technique, the wider and deeper the bucket).
- Second step is through the crotch of defender. Shoulders are staying parallel to the LOS.
- Outside foot is placed outside the defenders outside shoulder. Head is put to the outside of the defender and outside arm delivers a blow to same shoulder. With inside arm pull down on backside shoulder of defender to put his shoulders on different levels.
- If the defender fights reach and you cannot over take the block, rip with inside arm across the face of the defender and punch to the sky. Keep arm up and continue to sprint in the direction of the reach.

Coaching Points:
- Keep eyes to the sky and never stop running your feet.

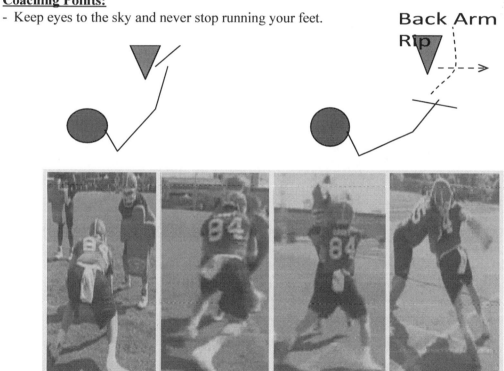

TIGHT END ROUTES, RELEASES, AND READS

Chad Walker, Linebackers Coach, Lafayette College

Purpose:

The purpose of this drill is to teach Tight Ends their routes, 1st and 2nd level releases, as well as sight adjustments reads on the routes they are running.

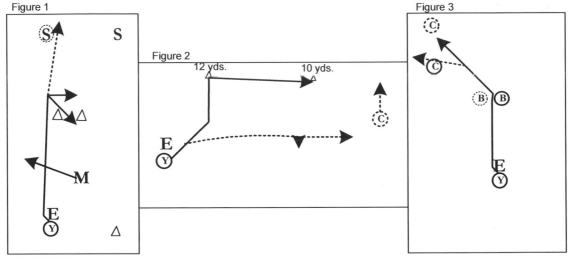

Coaching Points:

1. Use best release that is going to get you on the right path. Use a release move every time I/S or O/S.
2. Teach 1st and 2nd level releases (Rip, Swipe, Punch).
3. Run crisp clean routes. Teach body control.
4. Teach routes based on different zone and man coverage. When to sit and when to go?
5. Catch w/hands, tuck ball high and tight, finish up field.

Figure 1: Tight End uses I/S or O/S 1st level release based on DE's alignment. Pushes vertical up field using a 2nd level release to beat the LB. Gets eyes on safety, if safety is playing middle 1/3, TE should drop hips and hook or run window route at 12 yards. If safety is playing on hash in deep ½ or ¼ coverage, the TE should press the I/S shoulder of the safety and work toward M.O.F. opening. Catch, tuck, finish.

Figure 2: Tight End uses I/S or O/S 1st level release based on DE's alignment. If running drag, TE should push to seven yards across field, then push vertical up-field to 12 yards, stick foot in the ground and work across the field working downhill back to 10 yards. TE should stay square and show his #'s to QB if you are working on sprint out/naked. If running the shallow TE should push across field working to get depth at about 5-7 yards on the opposite sideline. If man is chasing continue to flat. If corner is sitting in flat, or there is another flat defender, TE should settle down showing his numbers to the QB in the open window of the zone defense. Catch, tuck, finish.

Figure 3: Tight End uses I/S or O/S 1st level release based on DE's alignment. Pushes vertical up field and works on 2nd level release vs. LB. TE should stick his foot in the ground, dip I/S shoulder, plant and push to 18 yd on SL. If corner is high in coverage in ¼'s TE should flatten route out. If TE is clouded TE continues to work to 18 yard landmark. Catch, tuck, finish.

TIGHT END 1ST AND 2ND LEVEL RELEASE DRILL

Chad Walker, Linebackers Coach, Lafayette College

Purpose:

The purpose of this drill is to teach Tight Ends their 1st and 2nd level releases.

Figure 1.

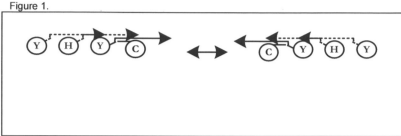

Figure 2.

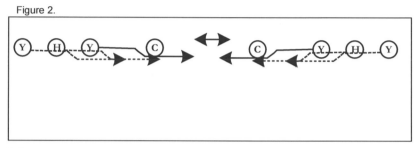

Coaching Points:

1. Teach proper technique with releases. (Rip, Swipe, Punch Over, Head Fake)
2. Teach proper footwork and body control.
3. Teach stacking defender and/or getting back on route path.
4. Do not teach swim move (exposes chest).

Figure 1: Tight Ends should be aligned 3 yards apart directly behind each other. Defender/ Coach starts in front of first TE. The TE should use release based on defender's alignment. Once he uses 1st level move he should clear his hips and then stack the defender and sprint 10 yards. The defender continues to move up field. Once he approaches the L.O.S. the next TE should go. This drill continues until everyone in the line has gone. Then the coach flips around and runs drill using opposite side release. This way you can fire out reps and work on releases to both sides.

Figure 2: Tight Ends should be aligned 3 yards apart directly behind each other. Tight End sprints toward defender/coach. The defender/coach tries to get hands on the TE and/or moves in a direction. The TE should execute his 2nd level release based on the defender. Once he uses his 2nd level he should clear his hips, stack defender and sprint 10 yards. The next TE should start to go once TE in front of him passes defender/coach. This drill continues until everyone in the line has gone. Then the coach flips around and runs drill using opposite side release. This way you can fire out reps and work on releases to both sides.

Note: You can add routes to this drill so the TE isn't always going straight ahead. You can also assign what release moves to use so they are practicing and learning the different techniques.

NOTES

QUARTERBACKS

QB FOOT WORK DRILLS
Curt Fitzpatrick, Offensive Coordinator, Utica College

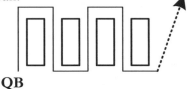

Snake Drill:

Purpose:
This drill works on a QB's movement within the pocket. You must emphasize short choppy steps when moving forward and back so that the QB remains in his "power position" at all times. On lateral movement, the QB's first lateral step must be with his back foot so that he is able to throw at all times.

Set-up:
4 agile bags, 1 football

Execution:
1. The QB should set up in a good passing posture at the top of his drop (eyes downfield, ball in proper carrying position, good ball security technique, etc.)
2. He should then start weaving through the bags using the fundamentals mentioned above. After a few reps one way, switch ends.
3. As a coach, keep verbally reminding him of the fundamentals incorporated into this drill. Also, check his ball security randomly by swatting at the ball.

Tennis Ball Pocket Movement:

Purpose:
To simulate a pass rush and make the QB react to the rush and move within the pocket. (You can also use this to simulate and escape movement as well.)

Set-up:
2 Tennis Balls, 1 Cone, 1 football

Execution:
1. The QB starts at the cone (center) and takes his desired drop.
2. Once at the top of his drop, he will set up with his eyes down field and in a good "passing posture."
3. The coach will then toss a tennis ball at the QB to his right or left to simulate a middle pass rush (or edge pass rush in the escape drill).
4. Once the QB avoids the rush have him make a short throw down the field.

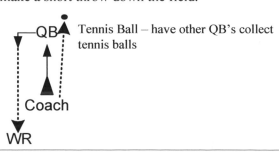

Tennis Ball – have other QB's collect tennis balls

QB WARM UP DRILLS

Mickey Fein, Offensive Coordinator, Lafayette College

THROW PROGRESSION:

Start with the QBs 10 yards away with their feet parallel. Make sure the QBs point their shoulder at the target and finish with their hand on the opposite hip like they are taking a dollar bill out of their pocket. Always have your eyes on the target and not on the ball. Then put your feet perpendicular to the line with your right foot forward and finish the same way. Then left foot forward. Once you get to 3 step, back them up to 15 yards and focus on the finish. The final part is to have them jog in place and have them throwing and jogging back and forth. Make sure when they are throwing on the run they start their motion with their throwing foot first. This will bring them to balance. This will get your QBs loose and ready for the day.

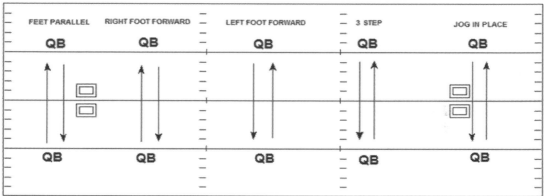

ZIG ZAG DRILL:

Start the QB at the sideline on one of the yard lines. Have him do a 5 step drop and then burst out of the pocket to his left. Make sure he spins out to his left if he is a righty and spins out to his right if he is a lefty. After the burst when he gets to the next 5 yard line have him 5 step drop again. Keep this going to the opposite hash. Then have him come back doing the same thing. Really works his feet and is a good conditioning drill.

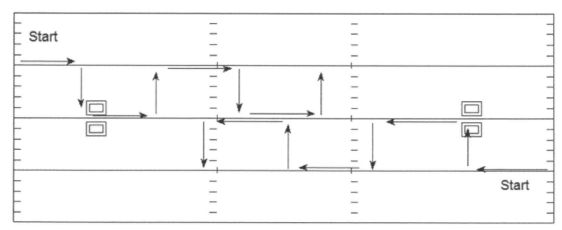

WINDOW DRILL

Kyle Cutnaw, Offensive Coordinator, Kenyon College

Purpose:
To teach QBs how to read open throwing lanes on horizontal or crossing routes.

Equipment:
1 football per QB, 1 receiver, 5-6 defenders

Description:
This drill is very helpful in teaching QBs how to see horizontal throwing lanes. The receiver will jog half speed across the field, simulating a crossing route. Spread the 5-6 defenders out across the field, facing the QB, with about 2-3 yards distance between each one. The defenders will take one big step to the right or left (they can choose or you can tell them). Once they take their step they must remain still (creates the open window). The QB will take a 5 step drop and try to throw the ball through the window to the receiver who is on the move.

Coaching Points:
- QB needs to execute proper throwing mechanics from the upper body.
- QB must adjust his back foot to ensure that the football is on target.
- Drill can be run from both directions.
- The throwing window should be different every time.

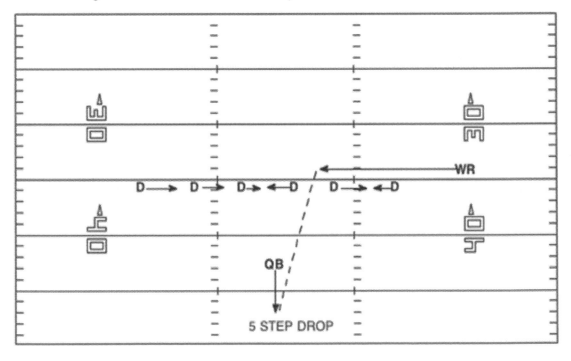

JETS DRILL

Scott Brisson, Offensive Coordinator, St. Lawrence University

Equipment:
8 cones spread out with the farthest one being 5 yards from the QB.

The QB will start in the middle of the cones as if he is at the top of his drop. The QB coach will direct the QB in various directions using his hands. The QB will then weave a figure eight around the indicated cones always keeping his front shoulder forward and always returning to the center starting point. When giving a lateral direction, the QB coach will include a "forward" or "backward" call with the point telling the QB which way to start his slide. The drill will finish with the QB back in the center and the QB coach yelling "throw" and pointing to the direction of the backup QB to throw to.

Coaching Points:

1. Keep eyes downfield.
2. Lead with the back foot and keep back knee flexion to always remain in a throwing position.
3. Use quick slide steps to get back to a throwing position quickly.
4. Keep ball in good carriage position to facilitate quick release.
5. Always throw from a balanced position.

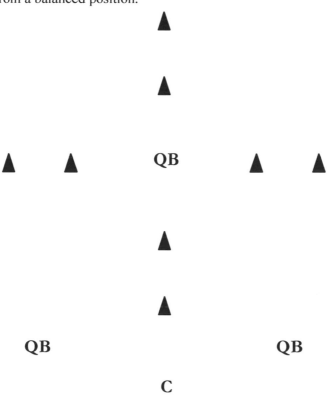

TRIPLE OPTION FUNDAMENTAL QB/FB PROGRESSION

Clayton Kendrick-Holmes, Head Football Coach, NY Maritime College

It is a privilege to have the opportunity to contribute to the first ever Lauren's First and Goal Drill Handbook. NY Maritime College started football from scratch in 2005 and we installed the Spread Triple Option which I learned while working for The US Naval Academy. You can use this same drill progression or make modification to fit your specific scheme. We use these drills during installation at the beginning of the season and during the season to address and correct any developing bad habits or problems that arise. I hope these basic drills with corresponding coaching points will make your players more effective.

#1- FIRST STEP DRILL:

Put your QB straddling a line with your FB 4-5 yards behind him. Place a cone or disc 4 feet on either side of the QB to represent the inside leg of the OG. Both players should be in their stances. QB calls the cadence and both the QB and the FB take their first step on the snap.

Coaching Points QB:

Pre Snap stance and eyes. QB must use correct tempo in his cadence as this controls motions and play timing. QB must get into his read position as fast as possible. QB must gain ground parallel to the LOS which can be seen by the line he is straddling. Feet must be staggered with front foot up, weight on inside balls of feet, knees and ankles bent with good power angles. Ball back as far as possible and at the right height vertically (QB arms parallel to the ground). Hips should still face down the LOS and not be twisted facing into backfield. Chin on his front shoulder and eyes on the location of the read key (coach) and not the FB. Speed of getting into this position is the KEY.

Coaching Points FB:

Pre Snap stance and eyes up. First step must be a short and quick step downhill and must be pointed at cone. Chest should be over knee and hands ready to run. Common mistakes are over striding on the first step, FB stepping under himself (not gaining ground or stepping laterally) and standing up on the snap. You can put a board in front of the FB if he has problems with over striding. The line is helpful as well for him to see where his foot is and should be.

TRIPLE OPTION FUNDAMENTAL QB/FB PROGRESSION

Clayton Kendrick-Holmes, Head Football Coach, NY Maritime College

#2 - HOOK UP DRILL:

We move to this drill only after FIRST STEP DRILL can be done perfectly. After taking the first step, the FB moves up to where the QB has the ball and puts the ball in his belly/chest with his arms closed over the ball in a "soft squeeze". The QB calls the cadence again and rides the FB as he runs his track through the mesh area and over his cone. Initially, we will pre-determine all gives and have the QB give the ball every time so they "get the feel" of this option. Next, we pre-determine all pulls so they "get the feel" of the pull phase. Finally, we move to a read phase and have the coach (who should be standing in the area of the read key) tell the QB by movement or hand signal whether to give or pull. The key to this drill is getting the QB and FB comfortable and confident when they are in the mesh. They are in close quarters and the QB should have the ball and his hands and arms deep in the belly/chest of the FB. This phase is the most critical part of the option as your QB makes his decision.

Coaching Points QB: QB must keep his eyes on the read key (coach) the entire time. Must shift his weight to his inside foot as the FB passes through. QB must push off his inside foot and step with his outside foot as the FB clears and accelerates out of the mesh toward his next read. During a give the QB should apply pressure on the ball with his front hand while pulling his back hand out. During a pull the QB must pull the ball out prior to the ball reaching his front hip. If the QB is ever in doubt of what decision to make he should give the ball.

Coaching Points FB: FB must accelerate through the mesh and stay on track. He must not slow down or cut during the mesh. FB must stay close to the QB in the mesh and maintain a "soft squeeze" on the ball for security. If the ball is in his belly when he gets to the front hip of the QB, he should take the football. If he doesn't get the football he should stay on track and look for a block. Do not stop running.

#3 - MESH DRILL:

This drill puts the whole QB/FB operation together. Go back to the starting point of FIRST STEP DRILL and on the QB cadence both players run through the entire mesh and decision process full speed. Initially, you can go back to all gives or pulls to get "the feel" from start to finish at full speed and then move to a decision process for the QB. We do this drill daily in season with the QB having to make a decision. The key to this drill is doing it full speed without ANY fumbles or wrong decisions.

Coaching Points QB: See all coaching points from previous drills. A primary mistake by QB's is not accelerating out of the mesh (especially without the football). A QB must carry out all fakes and even fake the pitch. The QB must not give up ground as he comes out of the mesh. It is important for him to accelerate "downhill" towards the inside shoulder of the Pitch Key. Do not give up ground out of the mesh!

Coaching Points for FB: It is the FB's job to get to where the QB has the football. If they are both taking their correct steps it should work out but the QB is looking at the key and not the FB. Other coaching points are the same as listed in previous drills.

*NY Maritime College has finished in the top 50 in rushing in each of its 4 seasons as a fledgling NCAA DIII football program. Since 2008 the team has finished in the top 10 nationally in rushing average using the spread triple option scheme. In 2009, NY Maritime College had its highest ranking at #4 with 316.4 yards per game.

DAILY DRILLS FOR ZONE READ PLAY

Dan Hunt, Offensive Coordinator, Colgate University

Ride/Decide Drill:

Quarterback starts with the ball in his hands. He wants to have the ball reached back, already seated in the belly of the RB. QB has his weight on his back foot. RB is 2 feet behind the QB. On the coach's command, the RB will press his assigned gap. QB will read the E as he steps and transfers his weight to his front foot. Coach can direct the E to go wherever he wants.

QB wants his hands reached back, his weight on his back foot. His front foot angled to the gap you want the TB in. He wants to step and transfer his weight to his front foot as he reads.

Next progression is to do the same drill, just with a snap from center.

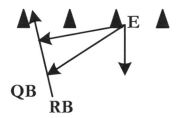

Second Level Feel Drill:

This drill helps the QB let the LB tell him what the E will do. It also develops feel for the RB as to where to put the ball. If the LB scrapes over the top, (1) the QB reads that as if the E has crashed down on the RB. The QB will pull and try to square up and get to the weak arm of the LB. If the LB steps straight up (2) the QB will read that as a feather DE and give the ball. The RB will feel the LB in the B gap and he will run through the A gap. If the LB shuffles inside (3) the QB will again read that as a feather DE and give the ball. This time the RB will bend behind the B and put the ball in the B gap. This drill can be done with or without a snap.

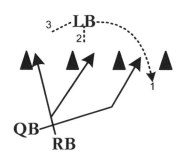

DAILY DRILLS FOR ZONE READ PLAY

Dan Hunt, Offensive Coordinator, Colgate University

Bang/Bend/Bounce Drill:

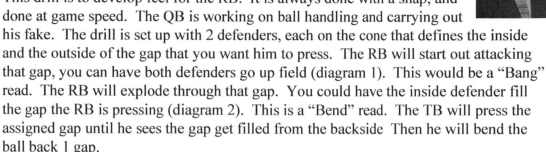

This drill is to develop feel for the RB. It is always done with a snap, and done at game speed. The QB is working on ball handling and carrying out his fake. The drill is set up with 2 defenders, each on the cone that defines the inside and the outside of the gap that you want him to press. The RB will start out attacking that gap, you can have both defenders go up field (diagram 1). This would be a "Bang" read. The RB will explode through that gap. You could have the inside defender fill the gap the RB is pressing (diagram 2). This is a "Bend" read. The TB will press the assigned gap until he sees the gap get filled from the backside Then he will bend the ball back 1 gap.

You can have the outside defender fill the assigned gap (diagram 3). This is a "Bounce" read. The RB will press his assigned gap until he sees it filled from the front side. Then he will bounce out 1 gap. It is important to stress to the RB to keep his hips square and press up field when he cuts.

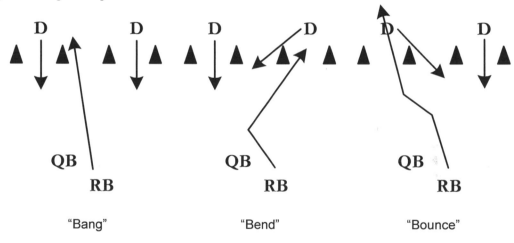

"Bang"   "Bend"   "Bounce"

NAKED BOOTLEG DRILL

Vinny Marino, Offensive Coordinator, Columbia University

When the QB runs a naked bootleg there are three scenarios that can take place and this drill will help prepare the QB for them. This drill can be done from under center or from the gun.

Scenario #1:

DE is flat down the line and chasing the RB.
Drill: QB makes hard play fake and sets depth and width outside the pocket. The QB will set his shoulders around and make the desired throw instructed by the coach.

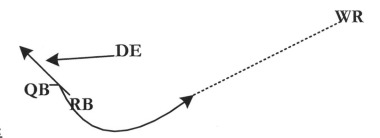

Scenario #2:

DE is hard up the field and boxes the QB inside.
Drill: QB makes hard play fake and works for depth and width. The DE has QB "Boxed" in so QB sets his feet and delivers the ball to pass receiver either in flat or on the over route.

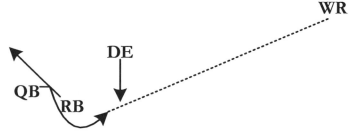

Scenario #3:

DE runs directly at the QB. QB has to decide whether to out run him to the outside or drop his foundation and deliver the ball quickly to the desired receiver.
Drill: QB makes hard fake and works for depth and width. The DE runs at the QB and the QB either makes a move on the DE to the sideline or the QB makes a move on the DE on the outside then drops his base and delivers the football to the desired receiver.

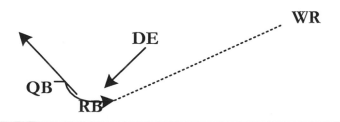

ESCAPE / TARGET DRILL

Mike Faragalli, Running Backs Coach, University of Virginia

Purpose/Coaching Points:

1. Teach QB's an awareness of pressure in the pocket.
2. Teach QB's how to "slide" in the pocket while keeping focus downfield on defense.
3. Teach QB's to maintain throwing position while sliding to avoid rush.
4. Teach QB's to keep front shoulder downfield while moving in the pocket, enabling a quick release to the target.
5. QB must move back foot first when moving in pocket. This enables quick release and prevents dropping ball and winding up, wasting time.

Execution:

- Have QB execute a 5 step drop, gather, feet moving, weight on balls of feet.
- Have coach or other person rush QB either with a high rush, forcing QB to step up or on inside rush forcing QB to slide outside.
- Line up 3 receivers as targets 10-15 yards downfield, 6-8 yards apart.
- As QB escapes rush, coach standing behind, points to one of the targets who then raises his arm.
- The QB must quickly step and throw to the target using proper fundamentals.
- Have rusher rush from QB blind side and passing side.

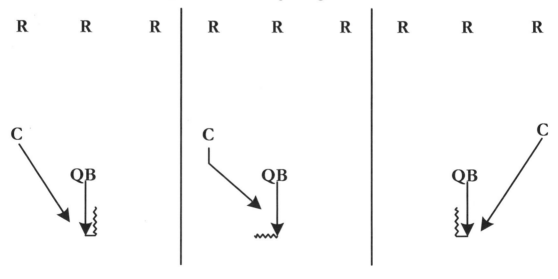

RUN-UP / ESCAPE DRILL

Michael Yurcich, Offensive Coordinator, Shippensburg University

It is our pleasure at Shippensburg University to share our drills with Lauren's First and Goal Foundation. The drill I will be featuring is the Run-Up / Escape Drill that we use to teach our QB's three important fundamentals – ball security, vision down field and launching while trying to escape / avoid pressure. The drills we practice are the drills that we witness our players performing as we watch game tape. The Run-Up / Escape Drill is one drill which we see over and over as we view our game film.

We can incorporate under center drops (5 step / 7 step) or gun drops (3 step / 5 quick) into the drill. We start by placing targets down field (you can use your favorite pattern progressions Fig. 0). Sometimes I will grab a kicker or manager to help if we are low on numbers. We also place two edge rushers on each edge of the pocket. If the rushers contain, we simply run-up and throw to which ever target the coach points to pre-snap (Fig. 1). If one of the rushers forces the QB to escape the pocket, we tell the QB to escape and throw to the coach point (Fig. 2). When the QB escapes to his off hand side (Rt handed QB - escape to the left) we incorporate the 10 YD rule (Fig. 3/4). The 10 YD rule: when escaping the pocket to off hand side- sprint 10 yards to separate -- if no chase - profile (set up) and throw ball to coach point (Fig. 4. While you sprint the 10 YDS to the left if you feel pursuit - stay on run and throw to coach point (Fig. 3. Have a 3rd defender in the drill to the QB's off hand side to simulate pursuit (Fig. 3) - or no pursuit (Fig. 4) so the QB can feel whether or not to profile / stay on the run.

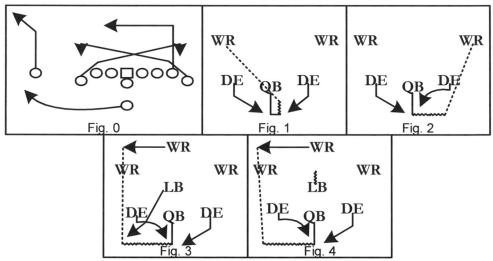

Fig. 0   Fig. 1   Fig. 2   Fig. 3   Fig. 4

The main coaching point we will stress throughout the drill is ball security. We will maintain a throwing grip, however, the QB is to have two hands on the ball until he separates to release the ball. We may incorporate a bag to try and jar the ball loose as the QB runs up or escapes. As the QB turns his body to escape we must make sure he keeps both hands on the ball as this is a susceptible movement enticing one hand ball insecurity! As the QB runs up in the pocket, we teach him to put the ball up on his front number in order to secure the ball as the DE reaches to strip from behind. I believe this drill teaches the QB sound fundamentals in order to secure the ball, see downfield/feel pursuit, and throw from awkward launch points

Shippensburg Football would like to thank the Lauren's First and Goal Foundation for their help in supporting families who have experienced childhood cancer. We are honored to have been a part of this year's drill manual. Thank you.

QUARTERBACK SCAN DRILL

Mike Sullivan, Quarterback Coach, New York Giants

Purpose:
- Develop QB's ability to go through proper progression to find open receiver.
- Emphasize QB proper set-up and reset of feet to throw ball to open receiver.
- Improve quickness of release once QB recognizes open receiver.

Execution:
- Position 3 WR'S 12-14 yards deep facing QB.
- WR's should be evenly distributed—1 directly over the ball and the other 2 inside the numbers.
- QB coach stands behind QB and points to a specific receiver who will be "open" during QB's scan.
- QB takes 5 step drop with a reset and begins scan left to right.
- Designated receiver indicates he's open by extending his hands—only doing this when QB makes eye contact with him.
- 3-4 reps going left to right, then repeat 3-4 reps going right to left.

* "Open" Receiver

WR   **WR**   **WR**

QB

Coach

NOTES:

1. Coach Point to receiver BEFORE QB starts drop so you can watch QB's feet/steps on drop.
2. You can add a 4th receiver, placing 2 in hook areas and other 2 six yards from S.L.

ESCAPE DRILL
Tom Doddy, Offensive Coordinator, Rowan University

Objective:
Teach QB to escape a free rusher off the edge.

Set Up:
Use one QB/Kicker to snap, one to rush, and one to stand out as the wide receiver. On the QB's cadence, the ball is snapped and the edge rusher attacks the inside or outside of the QB. The QB must use proper escape technique to elude the edge rusher. The QB will escape to the side of the free rusher and deliver the ball to the receiver. Work both sides in order to practice against blind side rushes also.

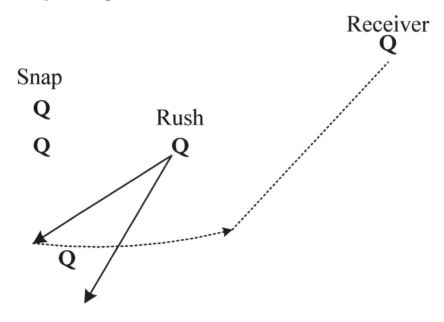

PROGRESSIVE-NO

Greg Roskos, Offensive Coordinator, SUNY Cortland

I would like to thank the Loose family and Lauren's First and Goal Foundation for this opportunity to contribute to a great cause. The drill I am going to explain and detail here is one that we do everyday with our quarterbacks. Every clinic that I have ever been to has always talked about making sure your drill work replicates what actually happens in a game. "Progressive-No" is designed to help a quarterback both go through his progression and also see the entire concept with no defenders in space. This drill can be fitted to any of the progression type pass concepts that are currently in your offense. We never talk primary or secondary routes in our offense. The defensive alignment/coverage will allow us to read the open receiver and to throw accordingly.

Drill Needs:
1 Manager/WR
5 Quarterbacks
1 Football

Example #1:
In the first example diagrammed below, we will line up our five "wide receivers/quarterbacks" at the end of each of the five routes. They are stationary targets.

WR #1 is simulating a deep out route and will stand 3 yards from the sideline and at a depth of 12 yards.

WR #2 is simulating our choice route and will stand 3 yards from the top of the numbers at 10 yards depth.

WR #3 is simulating our hunt route and will stand 8 yards from the LOS directly over the guard.

WR #4 is simulating our knife route and will stand 12 yards from the LOS directly over the opposite guard.

WR #5 is simulating our RB in an area route and will stand 3 x 3 from the opposite tackle.

The QB will take a 3-step drop from gun and plant his back foot to throw the deep out route (#1). The coach will stand behind the QB and off to the side. If the coach yells "No" before the QB has released the ball, he will reset his feet and throw to next WR. If the QB hears two "No's", then he throws to the 3rd WR. Three "No's" = #4 WR, four "No's" = #5 WR. We use this for several of our drop back pass concepts. We try to teach the QB to be ready to make every throw <u>unless</u> he hears a "No." A big coaching point is to make sure the QB always has his feet in good throwing position and the ball held high ready to reload and throw.

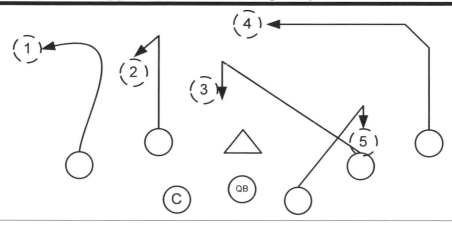

TRIPLE OPTION – 2 BALL DRILL

Brian Sheehan, Offensive Coordinator, Thomas Moore College

Purpose:

To efficiently teach player aiming points and develop feel for give, pull, keep and pitch when running the triple option.

Procedure:

1. Align quarterback, dive back and pitch player in desired backfield locations.
2. Align a center (C) to snap the primary football, a cone for dive back's aiming point, a player to serve as Handoff Key (P1), a second quarterback to hold a 2nd football (Q2), and a player to serve as Pitch Key (P2).
3. Prior to the snap, coach will signal the Handoff Key (P1) to force the give or pull and the Pitch Key (P2) to take quarterback or pitch player.
4. On the quarterback's cadence, players run basic triple option assignments. Dive back's path is set by the cone. Quarterback's path is set by 2nd quarterback. Pitch back's path is set by maintaining 1x4 (1 yard deep and 4 yard wide) relationship with quarterback.
5. If Handoff Key provides space for "give", quarterback will handoff to dive back and will take 2nd football from Q2 to attack the Pitch Key. If Handoff Key takes away space to force "pull", 2nd football will not be used.

Key points:

- Give the quarterback 1-way, unless rules for both dive and pitch. For example, "Hand the ball off every single time, *unless* the Handoff Key takes away space for the dive back to run."
- Players must work towards the "Option Alley" or play-side, outside 1/3 of the football field. This is especially important for quarterback and pitch player to work away from pursuit.
- Mix in "quick pitch" scenarios, such as Mesh Charges (Handoff Key and Pitch Key to mesh point) and Bird Stunts (Pitch Key for dive back).
- Assign a Finishing Point downfield for backs to carry the football to, or "look for work".

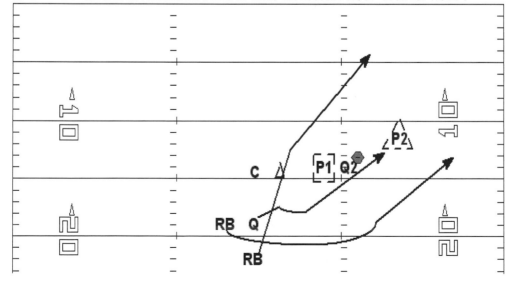

SOUTH FLORIDA SUMMER QUARTERBACK WORKOUTS

Peter Vaas, Quarterback Coach, University of South Florida

Exercise:
1. Fingertip Push-ups
2. Stretch Shoulders and back of arms
3. Jump Rope
4. Star Drill
5. Eye Exercises
6. Drop back over bags.   Vary distance between bags
7. Shuffle over bags-always initiating movement with back foot

Throwing Drills:
1. One Knee:
   Great shoulder rotation-on left Toe-Pull body through-start to get legs involved-exaggerate follow through by extending arm and finishing with fingers on the ground well in front of you.
2. Weight on left Foot:
   Be balanced on front of left foot with weight entirely off right foot-Get great shoulder rotation- Pull forward with left toes as right hip goes through the throw-get great follow through.
3. Step and Throw:
   Stand facing perpendicular to the target with a line going through your insteps-take a very small step slightly to the left of the line and throw the ball-shifting weight from right foot to the front of the left foot as the hips and shoulders rotate parallel to the ground-finish with your right hip having come around so your belly is square to the target-to slightly past square.
4. Increase Distance:
   Back up gradually-when can no longer throw ball on a flat trajectory then begin to drop back shoulder…ball will travel on plane of shoulders…still only take a short step and be sure to pull body up over left foot.
5. Throw On Run:
   Run at target and just prior to throw chop feet to gain balance-use same rotating of shoulders technique-should end up running directly at your target.

Target Practice:
Vary the distance of these throws as well as the height of the targets and the movement prior to the throw.

1. Drop and throw to a target.
2. Drop and throw to a target having to throw over an obstacle.
3. Throw a ball from the field to the top of the bleachers.
4. Throw a ball so it drops into a barrel.

SOLVE THE PROBLEM

Michael Canales, Offensive Coordinator, University of North Texas

QB executes either a 3 step drop from gun or 5 step drop from under center. Coach gives the QB a "Math Problem" to solve as QB is in his drop (i.e. $2 + 2 - 1$... Throw, $2 \times 5 - 7$... Throw). The QB solves the problem in his drop and throws to proper target. All pass concepts are based off keys or reads made by QB; this simulates game like situation forcing QB to think on the move.

I have a lot of fun with this drill and add a couple twists with it. I have used pass rushers for visual as well.

WR ⟶ **WR**   **WR**

QB

COACH

AVOID/RESET DRILLS

Jeff Behrman, Offensive Coordinator, Stony Brook University

(A) Reset Drill:

Objective: To maintain throwing platform, while having to reset feet in the pocket.

Procedure: Coach stands in front of the QB as he takes the snap and performs his drop. As the QB sets, the coach points either right, left, back or down in order to make him move in the appropriate direction. As he makes these movements, he is to go no more than three to four feet from his original set up. On the coach's signal, he sets his feet quickly ("Push – 1, 2") and throws the ball downfield to a target.

Variations:

Coach can use arm movements to communicate the rush.

Advance the drill by incorporating live rushers who rush at designated landmarks.

Coaching Points:

1. Check that he does not open hips and shoulders while resetting.
2. Do not raise up.
3. Avoid large steps.
4. Check that quarterback is keeping focus up field.
5. Do not stiffen the legs, keep flexion.
6. Check that quarterback steps with the back foot first.
7. Check that weight is on the balls of the feet with the majority on the back foot.

(B) Avoid / Reset Drill:

Objective: To improve pocket disciplines and increase unseen awareness by putting the quarterback into as many "pocket" situations as possible.

Procedure: The coach will determine the rush lanes by his arm movement before the drill is executed. If the outside rush shows, the arm movement is across the body. Starting always with the right outside rusher first, to the left outside rusher second, and finishing with the inside rusher. The first rusher will rush just underneath the quarterback's drop . When the QB has finished his drop and is in the pocket, he will be forced to move depending on the rush. The rusher will extend his inside arm, while running at outside shoulder for outside rush or extend outside arm while running at inside shoulder for inside rush. When #1 is ¾ of the way to the QB, #2 will rush the lane given by the coach. When #2 is ¾ to the QB, #3 will rush. The stagger is very important so the QB has time to react. The rusher must maintain his course and sprint all the way by the QB. At anytime during the drill, the coach will give a "BALL" call, telling the QB to set his feet and deliver the pass to the target.

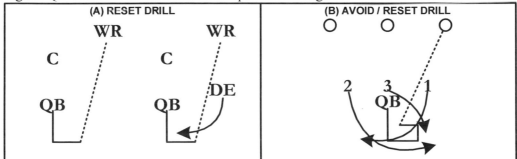

TRIPLE OPTION QB DECISION DRILL

Bryan Cook, Offensive Coordinator, California Polytechnic Institute

Drill Purpose:

1. Rapid fire repetitions of inside veer option fundamentals for QB/Fullback/Slot/ Center. Reads, Steps, and Timing.
2. Ball Security. Reinforce habits involving decision making, ball carrying techniques, and reactions to defenders.

Important Notes:

1. Line Strip must have exact dimensions to reinforce the correct track of the fullback QB mesh. Splits should be 3 feet.
2. Cadence must be rhythmical and consistent between QB's. "Down Set Go." Motion occurs on Set and the Center should anticipate the Go with the snap. The ball should hit the QB's hand on Go and the fullback should be rolling out of his stance on Go.

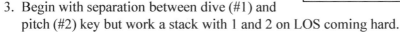

3. Begin with separation between dive (#1) and pitch (#2) key but work a stack with 1 and 2 on LOS coming hard.
4. Repeat to RT/LT sides and Field/Boundary. Include Center for realistic QB ball handling repetition.

QB Coaching Points:

1. Get first two steps down into the mesh. Get the ball as deep as possible to fullback transferring weight from back to front foot. Eyes are on the dive key. If 1 and 2 are stacked eyes should be in the B gap area seeing if either 1 or 2 steps inside for fullback.
2. Off the mesh the QB will take a clear step to avoid any collision by the DE into the fullback. The next movement is downhill into the defense on the crease. Attack and absorb the pitch key (#2). A flat pitch is a great pitch.
3. If you misread the dive key, NEVER pitch the ball off of #1 with #2 outside. Practice the reaction of sticking the foot in the ground and getting 2 yards off a misread.
4. Also to ensure the QB takes a snapshot of the slotback before pitching the ball, the coach will periodically hold the slot from going in motion so that the QB has no one to pitch to.

Fullback Coaching Points:

1. 70% of weight on front hand in a square sprinters stance. Lead step with the play side foot with nose on a track for inside leg of Guard. Should look like a sprinter takeoff for 5 yards, low and long.
2. Eyes are reading the block on the first play side DL. Inside elbow should be up with a soft roll on the ball. QB will push ball into belly in the event of a "Give Read." FB should stay on this track to the front pile-on unless defensive color crosses his face. He gets one cut, sticking outside foot in the ground and finishing straight vertical.

Slotback Coaching Points:

1. On "Set" the slot should get a step and a half motion on a line for the heels of the fullback. Burn it 3 steps past FB and mirror the QB. Notice 1-2 on LOS and be ready for hot pitch quick. Catch pitch moving downhill.

DROP AND DELIVER DRILL
Michael Behr, QB Coach, Moravian College

QB will start with a 5 step drop. He will then slide step to the right with pocket presence. QB will then slide step up in the pocket between the agility bags. He will then 5 step drop and continue the drill. When the coach raises his hands, the QB delivers the ball as quick as possible with his feet under him. This drill works on Pocket Presence, Footwork and Quick Release of the football.

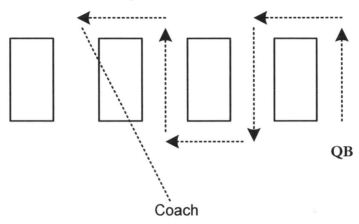

QB

Coach

QUARTERBACK DRILLS

Trey Brown, Quarterbacks Coach, Muhlenberg College

CIRCLE DRILL

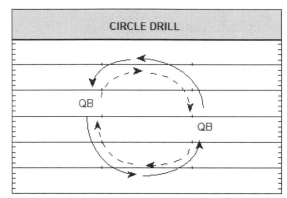

OFF BALANCE

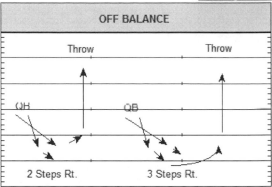

Two QBs should start 10 yards apart, with one QB holding a football. On the coaches command QBs start running clockwise and begin throwing the football. The coach will then stop them, and tell them to now work counter-clockwise. The drill is designed to get the QBs used to throwing on the run. The coach should check that the ball is being pushed deep into the back shoulder, and the front shoulder is pointed prior to release.

QBs should align 7-8 yards apart and be offset from one another. The coach should instruct each QB to take 2 or 3 steps to his right and deliver the football. He should then repeat the drill going to his left. The drill is used to simulate a QB attempting to sprint out vs. pressure coming off the edge. The QB actually may jump a slight bit as he attempts to get the football away. Extra follow-through and raised upper body torso are critical.

QUARTERBACK DRILLS

Trey Brown, Quarterbacks Coach, Muhlenberg College

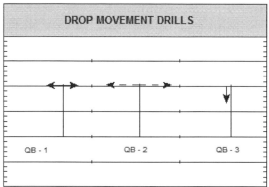

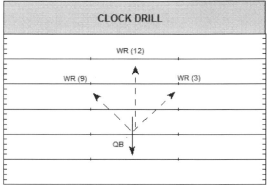

QB - 1 - Quick Shuffle - QB executes a 5 step drop. Coach gives the direction of the shuffle and the QB takes 2 quick steps. QB should keep front shoulder pointed downfield, and initiate movement with back foot. Incorporate a receiver to throw to.

QB - 2 - Long Shuffle - QB executes a 5 step drop. Coach gives the direction of the shuffle and the QB takes 4 steps. QB should keep front shoulder pointed downfield, and initiate movement with back foot. Incorporate a receiver to throw to.

QB - 3 - Step Up - QB executes a 5 step drop. Coach gives command to step up and avoid the rush. Incorporate a receiver to throw to.

QB will take a 3, 5, or 7 step drop. At the top of his drop a coach will call out 12 o'clock, 9 o'clock, 3 o'clock, etc., and the QB must step in that direction, pump fake, and step to the direction of the next call. Make sure QB is maintaining proper stance angle as he resets his feet before making pump fake.

NOTES

RUNNING BACKS

Photo by Michael Garner

ILLINOIS RUNNING BACK DRILLS

DeAndre Smith, Running Backs Coach, University of Illinois

Open Field Running Drill (Sideline)

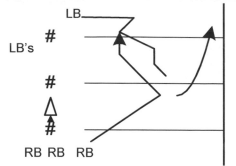

RB starts 10 yards away from a Defender, 10 yards from sideline. RB attacks Defender trying to beat him down the sideline, cutback or make a move. The Back must run full speed and cannot run over the Defender. The Defender separates, comes under control and tries to make the tackle.

Open Field (Middle of the Field)

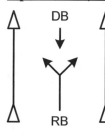

RB attacks Defender straight on and makes a move either way to score.

Fit Drill

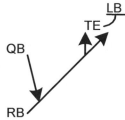

Work outside zone play. Read TE reach block. Make a cut and defeat the safety.

Defeat A Tackler

Hit & Spin

Start a RB and Defender 3-4 yds apart. Running back drives into Defender staying low, hits through the defender and spins off. Finish past a goal line.

Straight Arm

Start a RB and Defender 5 yds apart. RB runs to Defender and drives free hand to Defender's breast. Lock out elbow. Separates away from defender lifting knees to escape a tackle.

Hit & Rip

RB attacks Defender and rips arm through armpit of tackler. Stay low and run through the tackle.

ONE CUT DRILL

Dave Archer, Running Backs Coach, Cornell University

Purpose:

To condition the back to read a block, "stick his foot in the ground" and cut UP the field.

Procedure:

The Coach stands in the middle of the bags. As the back approaches him he leans in one direction. The back sees it and cuts the opposite way. This is a great drill for outside and inside zone runs. Make sure they finish through the finish cone up the field. Emphasize sharp cuts – do not round it!

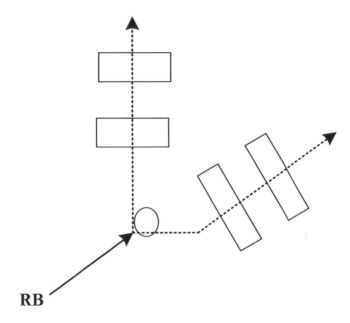

RB

RUNNING BACK GAUNTLET
Scot Dapp, Head Coach, Moravian College & Former AFCA President

There are numerous traits that a great running back possesses. We do not all have "great" running backs so we have to try to develop some of these traits in our "good" running backs. When you set up a drill for the RB's you want make sure the drill is working to develop / improve one or more of the traits that define a great RB. You can easily design a drill that totally emphasizes one individual skill; or design a drill that works on a combination of these traits or skills. I like these combination drills because they are more time efficient. Here is one I use on a regular basis.

Equipment: 2 light-weight standup dummies; 1 step-over bag; 1 hand shield; footballs.

Set up:
1. The RB stands at his normal depth from the LOS; another RB, extra QB, or even a manager will stand a few yards in front of the RB and off to one side. The coach will simulate the snap count and the RB explodes from his stance toward the LOS and receives the ball from the "QB".
> - *You are working the RB's stance & start and his proper hand position for receiving the football.*

2. Two extra RB's are at or near the LOS holding the standup dummies with about a 2-foot gap between the bags; as the RB approaches, the bag holders will "squeeze the gap" by leaning the bags toward each other. The RB must lower his shoulders to explode through the hole (bag holders need to be firm).
> - *You are working the RB's ball security and body position as he goes through the line (lower the shoulders and arms securing the ball to his chest); also looking for leg drive as he hits the dummies.*

3. Another player kneels down in a position a yard or two behind the dummy holders and off to one side; this player has a step-over bag and as the RB starts to clear the dummies, he slides the bag in front of the RB so he must step over the bag. The RB must drive through the hole and pick up his feet to step over any obstacle in front of him.
> - *You are working the RB's footwork (high step) and vision.*

4. Another player, holding a hand shield, stands anywhere from 5-8 yards from the LOS directly in the path of the RB. As the RB clears the step-over bag, this "defender" can attack the RB with the shield or hold his ground and feint one way or the other. As the RBs clear the step-over bag, he must react to the "defender" and make the appropriate move. If the defender attacks, lower a shoulder into the shield and work a spin move. If the defender holds his ground and feints in one direction, the RB must cut opposite his move.
> - *You are working the RB's ability to react to a second level defender in his path as he clears the LOS; he will have to work on an explosive shoulder drive and spin move; or a quick cut opposite the move of the defender.*

5. The RB finishes the drill by accelerating after his final move (spin or cut) and explodes up field 5 more yards.
> - *You are working acceleration and FINISHING.*

RUNNING BACK GAUNTLET

Scot Dapp, Head Coach, Moravian College & Former AFCA President

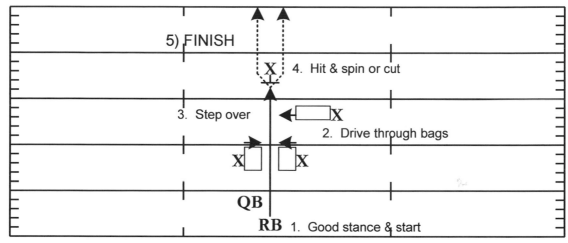

5) FINISH

4. Hit & spin or cut

3. Step over

2. Drive through bags

QB

RB 1. Good stance & start

RUNNING BACK DRILLS

Isaac Collins, Head Coach, Widener College

Open Field Running　　　　　　**DRILL: Stumble Drill**

Objectives:
To Teach Ball Security and Balance.

Line up RBs with footballs on goal line. On the coaches command, RB's begin running. At every five yard interval, the ball carrier must reach down and place palm of his off hand on the yard line, causing him to stumble. The ball carrier regains his balance, switches the ball to the opposite arm and executes the stumble technique until he reaches the 25 yard line.

Coaching Points:

- Players must place palm on designated line.
- Ball carrier should be instructed to raise his head up, stick his chest out and drive his knees forward to help him regain his balance.
- Make sure ball switch technique is executed properly.

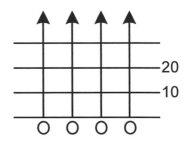

Ball Security　　　　　　**DRILL: Gauntlet**

Objectives:
To teach ball security and running with leverage.

- Place four to six men holding dummies approximately 1 yard apart staggered. On the cadence, the RB runs through the gauntlet while taking hand off from coach. The bag holders hit the ball carrier, trying to knock the ball loose, or knock him off balance.

Coaching Points:

- Take hand off properly and secure the ball.
- Make sure RB keeps his shoulders down and butt low for good leverage.
- RB should explode through the bags, maintaining a good high knee lift and keeping feet moving.
- The goal is to protect the football and stay on course.

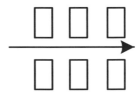

RUNNING BACK DRILLS

Isaac Collins, Head Coach, Widener College

Open Field Running: Ball Switch Drill   **DRILL: Ball Switch**

Objectives:
- To teach ball security in open field running.

Set Up:
- Align six cones staggered, five yards apart. RBs line up single file behind the first cone holding footballs. On the Coach's command, the first RB weaves through the cones. He must switch the ball to the outside arm to protect himself from a would-be tackler.

Coaching Points:
- The outside arm should reach over the top of the football.
- Both hands are used to guide the football to the outside armpit.
- The ball should be kept close to body during switch.
- The inside arm should be used to protect the ball carrier against on coming tackler.
- Stress ball security.

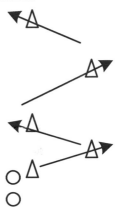

Running-back Blocking   **DRILL: Lock On Drill**

Objectives:
- To develop skills related to staying locked on a defender.

Set Up:
- One offensive player assumes the perfect fit position. On the Coach's command, one defensive player will move in the direction indicated by the Coach. The offensive player will lock on and maintain contact until whistle blows. This drill should be executed one pair at time.

Coaching Points:

- Keep butt down and head up.
- Fight pressure with pressure.
- Step in direction of movement.

BREAKOUT

Jay Mills, Head Coach, Charleston Southern University

Objective:

An all-encompassing drill for the ball carrier that combines the fundamentals of stance, start, pocket, exchange, vision, decision-making, ball security, and footwork.

Description:

1. Position six people in an inverted pyramid simulating the three levels of defense (DL, LB, DB). Each level defender is seven yards in depth and width from the preceding lower level defender.
2. Align running backs in stance at proper depth facing first defender.
3. The coach is stationed at the mesh point to hand the ball to the RB.
4. On snap count, the back takes off from his stance, executes an exchange with the coach, and proceeds towards the first defender. As the back approaches the first person, the defender will lean left or right. The back will break away from the defender's move and burst toward the next level defender. The process will repeat itself until the running back "breaks out" of the third level to the open field.
5. Drill should be conducted with exchanges occurring on both sides of the RB.

Coaching Points:

1. A proper balanced start should be observed prior to beginning the drill.
2. The back should begin the drill with correct first step and body lean.
3. Instruct ball carrier to keep his eyes focused on the defender while proceeding through the mesh point.
4. A pocket that insures a secure exchange should be emphasized.
5. The back should make his cut as close to the defender as possible.
6. Each redirection should encompass a solid plant foot placed directly under his hip and a corresponding lead step toward the next level (no crossover steps).
7. The ball should be secured with proper pressure points at all times. It should be kept under the arm in which the participant redirects. In switching the ball to the opposite arm, the open arm must come underneath to pull the ball across.
8. Tempo should be increased as techniques are mastered.
9. Drill concludes when the running back sprints past final line.

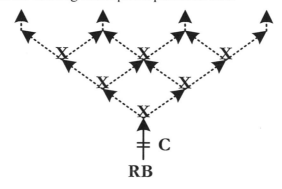

FINISH THE RUN

Christian Ozolins, Running Backs Coach, Buffalo State College

Objective:
To develop aggressive running style.

Drill:
1. Have one player with a shield about 5 yards away.
2. Have RB run at the shield (can catch a pass before).
3 The defender will give the RB a solid blow with a shield.
4. The RB, against the blow, will lower his hips and deliver his own rising blow to the defender by using same foot and shoulder.

Goals:
Ball Security
Violent Running
Yards after contact – "Finish your runs"

Equipment:
One Shield, Football

RB
RB
RB

Hop-Cut to Finish Drill:

Objective:
Quick feet and finish the run.

Drill:
Start with the ball, run to the first cone, hop with two feet, come back inside to the next cone, hop with two feet. Cut back and score. End the drill with a spin or a bag to score.

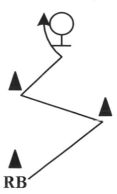

RB

BEND, BANG, AND BOUNCE

Tyrone Wheatley, Running Backs Coach, Syracuse University
Jason Vrable, Offensive Assistant, Syracuse University

EQUIPMENT:
Football, Agility Bags

INSTRUCTION:
These terms describe how the ball carrier enters the line of scrimmage.

COACHING POINT:
Teaches the ball carrier to enter the LOS with his shoulders square. Entering the LOS with shoulders square the ball carrier will press the LOS resulting in a Bend, Bang or Bounce.

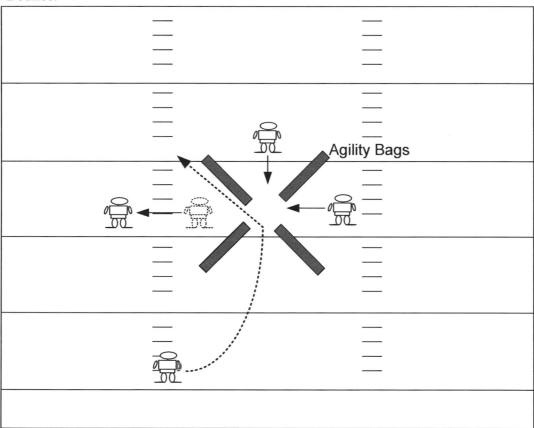

Agility Bags

RB PASS PRO PROGRESSION

Ryan Hess, Football Operations, Lafayette College

Pass protection technique is one of the most underrated abilities for a running back. With individual practice time being scarce to begin with, there are a few things you must emphasize in order to get the best results from your guys.

1. Head Placement
2. Hand Placement
3. Foot Placement

In order to get this to become second nature to your players these three points must be drilled into their heads during each drill.

Partner Punch:

Each running back partners up and stands across from one another about an arms length apart. Designate one side offense and one side defense and have the offensive player offset a half a man to the left (inside leverage). With each whistle the offensive player will make a 6" step with the near foot and punch. The near foot must split the crotch of the defender with the step while the punch aims for the chest plate. Elbows must be in while thumbs point to the sky. The strike will come from the heel of the palm. Repeat this five times and switch offense and defense, then go back and offset to the right.

Mirror Dodge with Pass Rush:

Set up two cones about three yards apart with an offensive and defensive player about an arms length apart in the middle. The running back offsets a half-man to the side of the quarterback. On the first whistle the defender moves back and forth between the cones forcing the running back to maintain leverage by shuffling back and forth, keeping his shoulders square. On the second whistle the defender attempts to put on a pass rush and attack the landmark of the QB. The running back must maintain inside leverage and use proper technique to stifle the pass rush.

QB

RB – LB 1 on 1's:

Running Back – Linebacker 1 on 1 has the linebackers start on the line of scrimmage in order to reduce contact on each of the positions. Starting on the right and moving to the left each LB will go with a different RB rotating in with each rep. Linebackers must make a move and are not allowed to bull rush. Coaches must emphasize inside leverage and hand placement for the running backs.

RUNNING BACK DECISION MAKING DRILLS

Jake DerCola, Running Backs Coach, Utica College

Pass Pro Decision Making:

Purpose:
Proper protection reads at full speed

Set up:
5 Bags, 4 Blitzers

Execution:
- The 5 bags act as the 5 linemen in their splits.
- The coach will make a protection call and stand behind the running backs and point to the blitzer who is coming.
- The RB must recognize who he is responsible for and, if his guy blitzes, execute the block. Otherwise, he will get to the proper check down.

Variations:
- Blitzers can move all around and start in different positions.
- You can send more than one blitzer and have the RB recognize most dangerous.

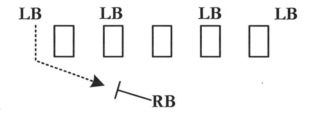

Daylight Run:

Purpose:
Reading the block and make a cut off of it

Set-up:
Stand-up dummies or guys with bags in a triangle formation

Execution:
- Drill will be set up in a triangle formation with blockers and defender at each corner.
- RB will run toward defender # 1 (at the point) and plant and cut opposite direction the defender indicates.
- Make sure the RB sets up the block. When the defender chooses a side, the RB should dip to that side to set up the OL's block even more.

Variations:
- Change the angle of the RB toward the first defender.
- After the first read, instead of having a another read, it can be a make a move in open field against defender.

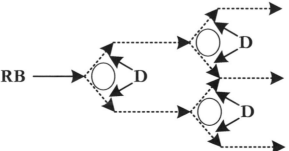

WIDE RECEIVERS

Photo by Mike Garner

UMASS WR DRILLS

Brian Christ, Wide Receivers Coach, University of Massachusetts

To become a great wide receiver you have to be able to stop and start Before the defensive back. Knowing and understanding how to do this is a critical part of route running. Many factors contribute to being able to "stop on a dime". Mostly it is a matter of controlling your body by using simple techniques. In these drills we will break down into small parts what happens at the point of a route when you need to stop.

The lower half of the body is the bigger and heavier half; therefore we need to stop this before we stop the upper half. The laws of motion say, "A body in motion stays in motion", that is why we want to try to slow down using our lower body and not our head and shoulders.

In this drill we want to have a series of cones placed in front of the receivers. The cones will be at 5 yard intervals. We will work on each phase of the break in small detail.

The first drill is to run straight through cones in as few steps as possible. Ask the receiver to stop by taking his nose to his toes, as if a sting runs from the end of his nose to his big toe. By slamming his foot into the ground it should pull that string which pulls his head and shoulders down. We want to always talk about stopping in this manner. When the receiver stops have him place his hand on top of the cone in the proper stopped position with knees bent, shoulders over toes, and arms in a running manner. The receiver should stay in this position until the coach commands him to go to the next cone. Then the next group goes. This continues all the way through to the finish line.

The next phase is to actually make a break. In this drill we are making a break back down the stem to the quarterback. Using the same cones and commands, the receiver will burst off the line to the first cone and stop in the exact same manner as the previous drill. Once again he will stay in the stopped position until the coach gives him the command. On the coaches command he will pivot on his up field foot and step with his back foot toward the line he just came from. We do this drill both ways, so the receiver has to stop on each foot and turn in each direction. After we have done the drill using the coaches commands we will let the receivers stop and go back on their own. One coaching point when the receivers are on their own is to not allow them to turn their feet or shoulders before they stop and touch the cone. We want everything to be square to that cone we are stopping on.

Now we progress to the stopping, coming back to the ball and exploding up field phase. Using the same cone grid, the receiver will explode off the ball slightly past the first cone. The receiver will stop in the correct manner and turn back to the quarterback as he did in the previous drill. We do not want to make a big circle as we come back. Also we want to keep our feet under our shoulders and not be over extended. Being over extended will make us slower out of our breaks and on our escape up the field. The receiver will go to the next cone and repeat the same mechanics.

All of these drills are done in both directions. There are designed to get a wide receiver's muscles to know how it feels to be in the correct position when they are stopping and starting. The faster and more efficient they are at controlling their bodies the better they will be able to create space away from the defender. The space created will be the difference between completion or an interception.

I hope these drills can be useful in developing your wide receivers. If we can ever do anything for you, please feel free to contact us at the University of Massachusetts.

UMASS WR DRILLS

Brian Christ, Wide Receivers Coach, University of Massachusetts

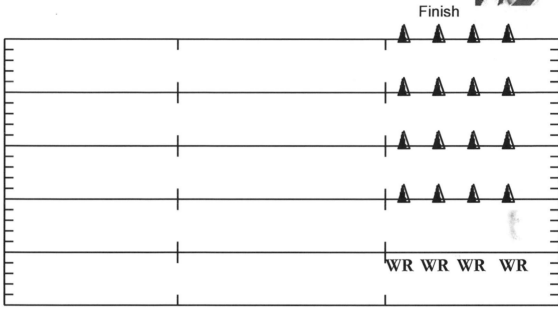

WIDE RECEIVER FOOTWORK DRILLS

Ari Confessor, Wide Receivers Coach, University of Rhode Island

Drive Drill:
1. Align 5 cones 5 yards apart.
2. Sprint to cone, back pedal around the cone.
3. Plant, stay tight, and accelerate to the next cone.
4. Work both sides. Right side of cone 1st, then left side.

Coaching points:
1. Entire drill should be done at full speed and with low center of gravity.
2. Drop hips when going around cone, keep shoulders square facing the next cone.
3. Accelerated arm action throughout drill.
4. After completing full 360º around cone, plant off outside foot and explode vertical to the next cone.
5. Stay tight around cone and eliminate extra steps.

Hip Drill:
1. Align 5 cones 5 yards apart.
2. Sprint to cone, complete tight 360º around the cone.
3. Plant, stay tight, and accelerate to the next cone.
4. Work both sides. Right side of cone 1st, then left side.

Coaching points:
1. Entire drill should be done at full speed and with low center of gravity.
2. Drop hips when going around cone, keep shoulders square facing the next cone.
3. Accelerated arm action throughout drill.
4. After completing full 360º around cone, plant off outside foot and explode vertical to the next cone.
5. Stay tight around cone and eliminate extra steps.

ARMY WIDE RECEIVER DRILLS

Tucker Waugh, Slot Backs Coach & Recruiting Coordinator, Army

Aggressive Shuffle Drill:

Purpose:

To learn the skill of moving quickly to attack your target while maintaining a shoulder-width base at all times for balance and power.

Coaching Points:

There should be an imaginary shoulder-width broomstick between your ankles. Side to side and forward movement will be directed by coach.

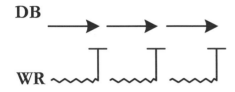

WR   WR   WR

C

* Coach will dictate lateral or forward movement by pointing. This is an intense tempo.

Shuffle and Pop Drill:

Purpose:

To simulate a lateral shuffle situation. The simulation of a blow-delivery increases the ability of the receiver to focus and hit a target while moving.

Coaching Points:

The feet should never come tighter or wider than shoulder-width. Strike with proper thumbs-up placement on the breastplate of the opponent.

DB

WR

* This drill should be executed at 3/4 speed to get the perfect fit position on the defender with each "pop."

Take the Battle to Him Drill:

Purpose:

We are simulating the situation where both the defender and receiver have settled. The defender to break on the football - the receiver to control himself and block. In this position, we will use this drill to teach the receiver transitioning from a reactive thought process to an aggressive one.

Coaching Points:

Coach will stand behind the receiver and indicate one of three directions for the defender to move. On a "GO" call, the defender will break, and the receiver will aggressively intersect him while keeping his shoulders parallel to the line of scrimmage. An initial strike takes place, and the drill concludes on coach's command.

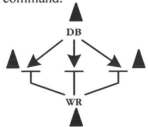

WIDE RECEIVER CONCENTRATION DRILL

Erik Scott, Wide Receiver Coach, William Paterson University

Objective:
This drill helps the receiver focus on the ball while eliminating distractions.

Frequency:
One to two times a week in training camp or more often if receivers begin to lose focus and concentration.

Relativity to the Game:
Helps receivers pick up the ball while eliminating unwanted stimuli.

Description:
1. Receiver lines up on the hash 10 yards deep from the thrower.
2. Have two other receivers three yards apart in the middle of the field.
3. As the receiver runs a crossing route have three balls thrown simultaneously.

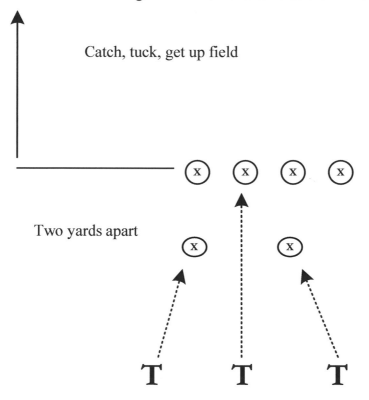

BALL DRILLS

Rick Ulrich, Wide Receivers Coach, University of Pennsylvania

Warm Up Throw

- 1 line of receivers
- Space to 20 yards

Catching balls ½ to ¾ speed

1. Out in front – 2 yards
2. 1 hand – emphasize eyes to tuck
3. Defense on inside hip
4. Turn front – ball thrown to point
5. Ball thrown over top

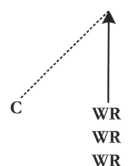

Over the Middle

- Work out of dig/drag/middle/cruise
- Back up net or fence
- Thrown from 15-25 yards
- Speed out of break

Work last 1-2 steps to cut then speed out of cut. Focus on arms moving then slowly as you react to ball thrown.
1. Put ball on time out of break
2. Let receiver pass to "next" open zone
3. Balls high/low/front/behind
4. Throw with defender distraction

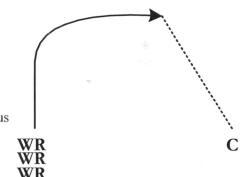

Attack the Ball

- Receiver aggressively comes down line chokes motor on ball thrown
- Ball is thrown from start to 20 yards at cone (should be caught with "feet alive")
- Turn right out of catch (the left)

1. Directs receivers 90 to right/left
2. Pop-glide M/M shake before direction
3. Defender chases

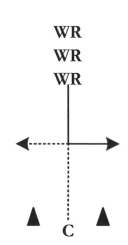

WIDE RECEIVER DRILLS

Jake DerCola, Wide Receivers Coach, Utica College

Ball Drills – Distraction Drills:

Purpose: Help receiver concentrate before catch.

Equipment Needed: Cones and football

Drill #1:

1. Have two lines 10 yards apart 2 yards deep.
2. Throw the ball as Def runs by Off.
3. Tell Def not to knock ball down, just distract.
4. Switch lines when complete.
5. Works well for balls across middle.

Drill #2:

1. Have two lines side by side with Def inside Off.
2. Throw ball over Def to Off – Same rules as above.
3. Works well for over the shoulder catches on verticals.

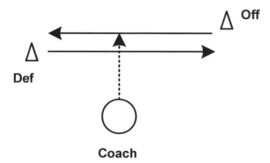

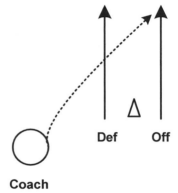

Cone Drills - Square Drill:

Purpose: Work on break point mechanics for various breaks (Curl, Dig, Sit, Out, etc.)

Equipment Needed: 4 Cones in a shape of a square.

1. Release to Cone #2, make a 90 degree cut for Cone #3.
2. Be ready for ball at any time after first cut.
3. Make a 90 degree cut for Cone #4.
4. Make a 90 degree cut for Cone #1 – Finish strong.

Variations:

- Alternate starting directions
- Have player stop for Curl route after 90° cut.
- Have players begin by breaking at 45 degree
- Sit routes.

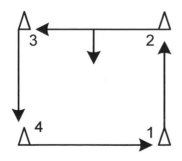

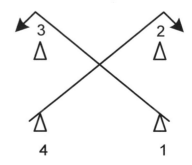

WIDE RECEIVER DRILLS
Jake DerCola, Wide Receivers Coach, Utica College

"Crib it" Drill (Catch the ball & take it to the "Crib"):

Purpose:
Works on the receiver's footwork at the top of his route, and also emphasizes finishing the play with yards after catch (YAC).

Equipment:
A cone, football
1. Decide which route to run.
2. From the cone, run the last phase of the route.
3. Work on break mechanics of route.
4. After catch, finish catch and get up field.

Variations:
- Work it both directions.
- Works best with all routes.

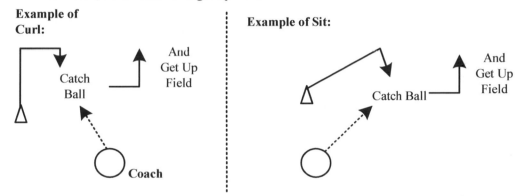

Example of Curl:
And Get Up Field
Catch Ball
Coach

Example of Sit:
And Get Up Field
Catch Ball

Tunnel Blocking Drill:

Purpose:
To work on stalk blocking both in space and while already in a "fit" with the defender.
Equipment:
6 cones, 1 football
1. Set the "tunnel" up with the 6 cones. It should be 15 yards long and 5-7 yards wide.
2. 2 blockers & 2 defenders (1st blocker in a fit w/ defender, 2nd blocker is 5 yards away from defender.
3. On "Go" RB tries to score and defenders try to defeat the blocks and make the tackle.

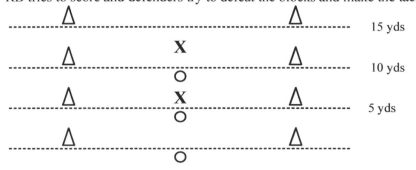

15 yds

10 yds

5 yds

ILLINOIS WIDE RECEIVER DRILLS

Paul Petrino, Offensive Coordinator, University of Illinois

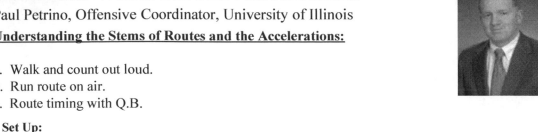

Understanding the Stems of Routes and the Accelerations:

a. Walk and count out loud.
b. Run route on air.
c. Route timing with Q.B.

Set Up:

Curl #1	Curl #2	Curl #3
5-4 Stem	4-5 Stem	3-6 Stem

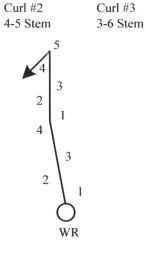

Procedure:

Receiver walks (progresses to run) pumping his arms-maintaining forward lean and counts out loud the steps.

        Curl #1- 1-2-3-4-"5" (emphasize acceleration)
        1-2-3-"4" (emphasize break point)
        Curl #2- 1-2-3-4 (accelerate)- 1-2-3-4-"5" (break point)
        Curl #3- 1-2-3 (accelerate)- 1-2-3-4-5-6 (break point)

Coaching Points:

a. Get to stride (no choppy steps).
b. Taint angle on your stems.
c. Eyes up, looking past corner.
d. Always finish route at the corner.
e. Pump your arms on the break.
f. On curl-step back at 45 degree angle to Q.B.
g. On curl at end of 2nd stem look inside to see underneath coverage.

Jam Corner
1. Stem Release
2. Slip Release

ILLINOIS WIDE RECEIVER DRILLS

Paul Petrino, Offensive Coordinator, University of Illinois

Tunnel Drill:

To develop concentration on the football and tuck the ball away to maintain possession of it.

Set Up:

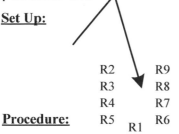

Passer (The Passer should be 15 yards from the Receiver)

Procedure:

1 Receiver will be designated the catcher. The remaining Receivers will align making a tunnel about 2 yards in between them. The catcher will take 3 steps. Plant and run into the tunnel to make the catch. After the catch he will tuck the ball, turn and run out the same way he came in. The passer will throw the ball at different heights. The receivers making the tunnel will have their hands in front of the football and then try to knock the ball out of the catcher's hands once he makes the catch.

Coaching Points:

a. Plant and run into the tunnel just like you were running a route.
b. Go to the football.
c. Concentrate on the football.
d. Look the ball in – tuck it away quickly and tightly and run out of the tunnel.

RUN AFTER CATCH DRILLS

Adam Lechtenberg, Quarterbacks Coach, Central Connecticut State University

Rip Technique:

Purpose:
An effective weapon to score the football while initiating contact with a defender.

Procedure:
Align 3 defenders in a row 5 yards a part. The defenders will hold hand shields at waist to chest height in a good football position. The receiver will execute a called route and initiate contact with the inside forearm and shoulder.

Coaching Points:
- Pad under defenders pad.
- Aggressively strike forearm in an upward motion.
- Drive and accelerate feet on contact.

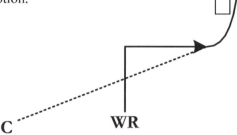

Stiff Arm Technique:

Purpose:
Effective technique to score the football when trying to turn the corner.

Procedure:
Align a defender 5 yards from the receiver and 10 yards from the sideline. The receiver will try and turn the corner on the DB, when the DB gets 1 ½ - 2 yards away the receiver will punch the DB in the center of the chest to fend him off.

Coaching Points:
- Aggressively strike defender in chest with an open hand.
- Accelerate and score the ball after making contact.
- Alternate sides.

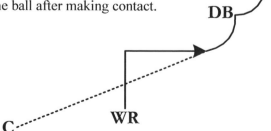

WR BREAK DRILLS
Kevin Cahill, Wide Receivers Coach, University of Maine

45 Degree Cut Drill:
WR will accelerate out of his stance bursting for set yards (5-8). Stick a break
point (3 steps) and angle to the far cone through center. Stick a break point
(3 Steps) and angle to top cone. Stick a break point (3 Steps) and angle to far
cone through center. Stick a break point and accelerate out of cones, look for ball from coach.
Do drill both ways.

Coaching Points:
Break point: eyes up, shoulders over toes, hands stay busy (Beat the Drums), accelerate out of
each break.

End Of Drill:
Throw a football, tennis ball, give them a line to finish through.

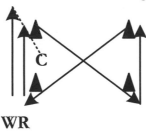

90 Degree Cut Drill:
Same set up as 45 degree: Now 1 step stick 90 degrees around each cone. Vary 1 step
and 3 step sticks. Speed cuts for 1 step, same break point mechanics for 3 steps.

Coaching Points:
Break point: eyes up, shoulders over toes, hands stay busy (Beat the Drums), accelerate
out of each break.

End Of Drill:
Throw a football, tennis ball, give them a line to finish through.

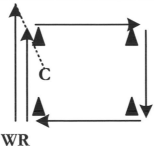

PRESS RELEASE ON BAGS
Powell Miller, Wide Receivers Coach, Widener University

Stem vs. Press on Bag:

Objectives:
- Teach proper outside stem release
- Emphasize importance of not getting jammed and getting a clean release

Procedure:
- Align on first bag head up. Use proper hand and swim technique to release outside.
- Repeat step one on bag number two that is 7 yards away and inside bag #1.
- Repeat steps 1 and 2 on bag #3 that is 7 yards away.
- Once one player is past the first bag, the second player is to start on the previous bag to begin the drill.

Coaching Points:
- Shoulder over knees over toes.
- Good back knee bend.
- Inside hand/arm back, outside hand/arm up and ready. We are in a sprinters stance with our arms.
- Good hand placement for release, good swim move and good first step to align for success.

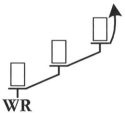

Release & Stack:

Objectives:
- Teach proper free release and foot fire technique. Then stack the defender from the LOS or the defenders catch technique.
- Emphasize importance of not getting jammed and getting a clean release and beating the defender from the LOS or his catch technique. Getting skinny and leaning back on the defender.

Procedure:
- Align bag head up. Use proper foot fire and hand/ swim technique. Release while getting skinny and leaning back on defender/ bag and then working to get on top of him.

Coaching Points:
- Proper foot fire technique and not being down the middle of the defender. Make defender choose a side.
- Good lean back on the defender to help create separation.
- Beat the defender with speed and then get skinny with your shoulders from the line and get on top of him.

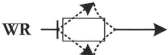

RED LIGHT – GREEN LIGHT DRILL

Ryan Roeder, Tight Ends Coach, Princeton University

DRILL:

The coach stands in front of the players 20-25 yards away from starting line. You will assign the WR's a specific route before they start each repetition. For example, the coach can instruct the players to run a comeback. You must also tell the players which direction to break the route.

The coach then starts the drill by saying go (or simulating a snap) and then raises both of his hands in the air. As long as the coach has his hands in the air, the players keep attacking vertically. When you drop both your hands, the players then break off to the designated route. The players must quickly transition to the appropriate stem while running full speed. The drill is done without a football and just focuses on route running. Multiple players can take a rep at the same time The drill can be used for any route in your offense.

PURPOSE:

The drill is designed to train WR's and TE's to have great vertical demeanor as they release from the line of scrimmage. The drill is also designed for them to practice breaking down quickly and **getting in and out of cuts while running full speed.** The players do not know when the coach will drop his hands so they must run full speed and cannot develop the bad habits that cause a player to telegraph his route. (Raising up, slowing arm action, etc.)

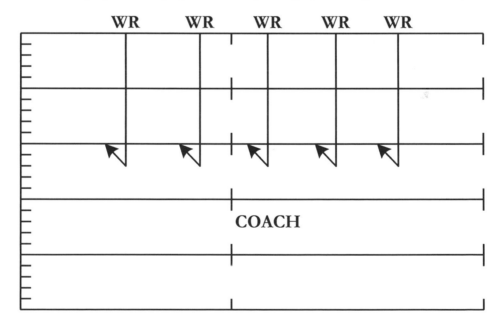

The direction to the players is to run a comeback breaking to their right. Players run vertical route until coach drops his hands. After the drill is completed, the players stay where they are and the coach jogs to other side to save time. The coach assigns a different route each rep.

WIDE RECEIVER DRILLS

Al McCray, Wide Receivers Coach, Fort Hays State University

Vertical / Leverage:

Objective:
To improve stance and starts.

Description:
Have the Receiver stand in a proper stance, and run toward the cone. Start off by having him run straight to the cone. Then place the cone at a 45 degree angle and have him run to it.

Coaching Points:
1. Make sure the Receiver is in a proper stance, ready to attack the Defensive Back's technique.
2. When the Receiver takes his first step, his arms should be in a good running form, making the DB think that he is going vertical.
3. The WR's first step should be at the DB, making sure he breaks his technique.
4. There will be times when you will not have to attack the DB's technique.
5. Make sure the WR comes off the line with low pad level (**DON'T SHOW YOUR NUMBER).**
6. Eyes up when you come off the line.

In Traffic:

Objective:
To teach wide receivers how to catch a ball in traffic.

Description:
Have two wide receivers hold the stand-up dummies. The stand-up dummies should be placed parallel to each other about four feet apart. While the wide out is running in between the stand-up dummies, have the receivers holding them hit the person running between them. The coach will throw the ball to the wide receiver while he is running in between the dummies.

Coaching Points:
1. Keep your eyes on the ball at all times.
2. Look the ball all the way into the pocket.
3. Protect your body after the catch. (Brace for impact)
4. Focus on the white lines on the ball.

DROP STEP & GET VERTICAL

Mike Hatcher, Wide Receivers Coach, Ithaca College

For this drill the WR will use a route release or top of the route technique to fit in between the cones. Once the ball is caught and secured the WR will drop step either of his feet Perpendicular to the LOS. He will then sprint through the bag holders.

As the WR's become better at this footwork, the Coach can throw the ball toward a specific side of the WR's and have them drop in the direction the ball leads them. The WR's are working on gaining ground up the field with their first step, while also trying to get their hips vertical. This footwork can help WR's become more efficient in situations where they are catching a ball in front of defenders and trying to split them up the field vertically.

Skills Worked:

Top of Route
Catch & Run Footwork
Ball Security

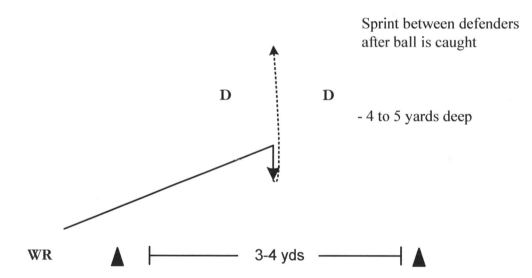

Sprint between defenders after ball is caught

D   D

- 4 to 5 yards deep

WR   ▲ |——— 3-4 yds ———| ▲

WR BALL DRILLS

Rob Moore, Wide Receivers Coach, Syracuse University
Jason Vrable, Offensive Assistant, Syracuse University

Catch and Post:

Player runs top of route, comes back to ball. Once player catches ball he will fake with head and shoulders one way and go the opposite way, finishing another 5 yards.

Coaching Point:
Make sure player keeps eye on the ball, as there is a tendency for player to look away from the ball to make his head and shoulders move. Also, player should be able to snap out of it.

Equipment:
1 Cone, Ball, Player

Open Hip Drill (Balls Behind):

Player runs top of route, then accelerates across middle or to sideline, ball is thrown to receivers back shoulder (behind), receiver opens hip to make catch.

Coaching Point:
Player must leave his feet to be able open his hip and reach behind.

Equipment:
1 Cone, Ball, Player

Sideline Drag:
As soon as player has control of football, which ever foot is down the other foot is dragged before going out of bounds.

Instructions:
Receiver runs top of route, then sprints to the sideline trying to keep both feet in bounds.

Equipment:
1 Cone, Ball, Player

WR BLOCKING DRILLS

Darrell Hazell, Head Coach, Kent State University

3 Bag Triangle Cut:

Align 3 stand-up dummies in a triangle. Receiver should attack the dummy six inches above the knee. Drive the near arm through the contact spot with his body square to the bag. He should explode through the dummy, land flat on his stomach and bounce back up. Repeat on dummy 2 and 3.

Coaching Points:

Receiver should be low and explosive. Head should raise on contact. Receiver must be close enough where he can step on the defender's toes.

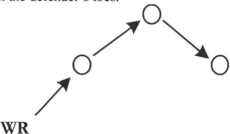

Push and Crack:

Receiver drives defender #1 off as he eyes defender #2. He must be under control on defender #1 in case he does not back off. If defender #1 backs out and #2 supports the run, the receiver must take an angle to intersect defender #2.

Coaching Points:

Receiver must have head-up to inside leverage on defender #1. This will enable him to get back to defender #2. Receiver may have to come back down hill to get him. Receiver must push off the ball so he doesn't have double support.

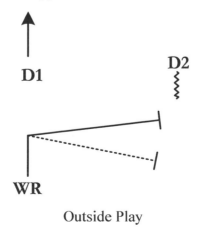

Outside Play

SCRAMBLE DRILL

Mike McCall, Offensive Coordinator, Northwestern University
Bob Heffner, Superbacks Coach, Northwestern University

At Northwestern, we run our scramble drill every day at practice. It allows us to practice several different aspects of our game on air. We use this drill for Conditioning, while also giving our guys mental and physical reps of our different plays, tempos, and snap counts. It gives the quarterback work on off rhythm footwork and throwing mechanics while working with the receivers. Probably the best thing it does is force our guys to focus when tired.

Set-up:
We get three groups together of just skill players (four if possible), with any left over players working in with the last group. The first group gets up, runs their play. We move the ball down the field working from the 5 to the 35 yard line with all 3 groups and then come back in from the 35 towards the GL. Depending on what you wish to emphasize in the period any play can be run (drop back, play action, etc.) at any tempo (huddle, no huddle, or "check with me").

Rules:
Play is called and the offense runs the play called. When they get their head around out of their break and see the quarterback breaking out of the pocket, they use these three simple rules to determine where they have to get to:

1. If you are on the opposite side of the field of where the quarterback is scrambling to stay at current depth then run straight across the field to get into the quarterback's vision as fast as possible.
2. If you are deep and outside of the numbers to the side of the scramble, come back toward the quarterback and stay tight to the sideline.
3. If are you shallow and outside of the numbers to the side of the scramble, go deep and stay on the numbers.

*** It is very important that your deep and shallow players outside the numbers stick to their landmarks so they can pass each other without an issue.

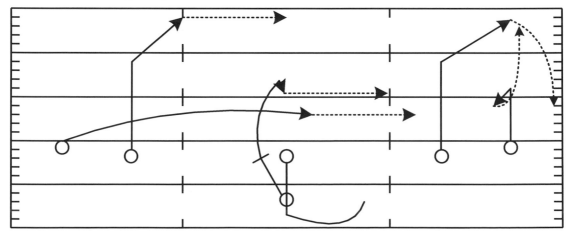

WR BALL DRILLS
Tripp Billingsley, WR Coach, University of Richmond

BAG DASH

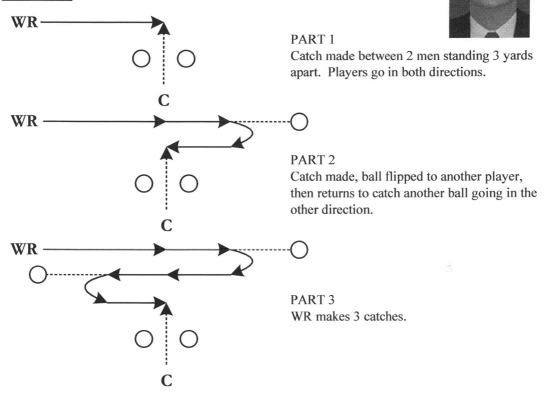

PART 1
Catch made between 2 men standing 3 yards apart. Players go in both directions.

PART 2
Catch made, ball flipped to another player, then returns to catch another ball going in the other direction.

PART 3
WR makes 3 catches.

NOTES:

WRs are to stay on the same yard line for each leg of the drill. Do not drift.

If time allows do a 4-catch.

GOAL:

Develop the ability to catch the ball with the hands while maintaining a flat route top.

WIDE RECEIVER DRILLS

Matt Hanhold, Wide Receivers Coach, Buffalo State College

Foot Fire Cone Drill

Four Cone Tunnel Drill

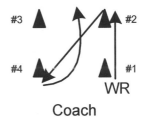

This drill is used to teach wide receivers proper footwork when defeating press coverage. Set up five to six cones to shape a W. Have the wide receiver work in a good shoulder width stance and patter his feet to each cone. Always emphasize low pad level and eyes up. Have the receiver keep his arms pumping in a narrow hallway. Work to each cone and finish with a 5 yard burst. You can also incorporate a football as needed. Emphasis on hips, eyes, arms and feet. Defeat the press.

This simple drill emphasizes coming out of a break, working back to the ball, and cutting to work back up field to the outside. The wide receiver will start at cone # 1 and work parallel to the cones, and at the top of the second cone settle their hips down and cut through the "tunnel". The coach will then throw the ball to the wide receiver, once the ball is caught the wide receiver will plant and turn outside cutting up field inside of the "tunnel". Point of emphasis: To teach receiver to keep cuts sharp, not to round off routes, and work to the outside after catching the football. This is very good for teaching the top of the route, working to the outside after the catch, especially on three step routes.

Cones #1 and #4 should be placed on hash marks. Cones #2 and #3 should be 2-3 yards away from #1 and #4 aligned with the hash.

WIDE RECEIVER DRILLS

Matt Hanhold, Wide Receivers Coach, Buffalo State College

Mirror Drill

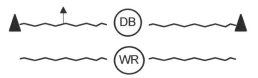

Mirror Punch Drill

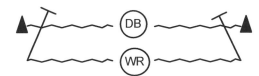

This drill is part of a stalk block progression teaching the receiver proper blocking technique. Place 2 cones 5 yards apart, with a defender standing in between them. Your receiver should be about 1 yard away from the defender. On the command of the coach the defender will work back and forth from cone to cone with a controlled movement. Prior to the command the receiver will be in the attack position with his knees bent and his chest up. His head should be up with his eyes picking out a point on the defender and mirroring the movement of the defender as he works from cone to cone. The receiver should have his feet at shoulder width apart and should never cross over his feet. Emphasize a good base. The receiver should always have his hands up in an aggressive attacking position, waiting for the opportunity to block.

This drill is the second part of a stalk block progression. Follow the directions for the mirror drill and on the coaches command the receiver will now engage the defender working his stalk block technique. Hands should be shot from the attacking position on the breast plate of the defender. Hands should always be inside. The goal should be to lift the shoulder pads into the throat or grab some cloth where it is not visible. The receiver will maintain his wide base, so if the defender gets loose, he will be able to mirror the defender again. Drive the defender through five yards and roll hips. This is done aggressively.

Grace & Lauren Loose along with Luke Ronco pose with
Coach Ted Daisher and Coach John Harbaugh

Long time professional and college
Head Football Coach, Bobby Ross
with Lauren at the inaugural camp

Lauren with Super Bowl MVP Phil Simms

Lauren with decorated Army
Officer and Coach, Ben Kotwica

Lauren and Maryland Head Coach Randy Edsall

Navy Head Coach Ken Niumatalolo and Lauren

Tampa Bay Buccaneers Head Coach
Raheem Morris and Justen Jones

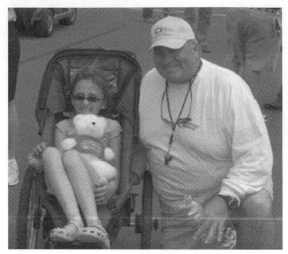

Lauren with Leo Govoni, Director of The Center
for Special Needs Trust Administration

Franklin & Marshall Head Coach,
John Troxell with Lauren

Grace & Lauren Loose with OSU Head Coach Jim Tressel

Former Lafayette and current NFL LB,
Blake Costanzo and Lauren

Lauren with Albany State Head Coach, Bob
Ford and Moravian Head Coach, Scot Dapp

John Loose, Otterbein Head Coach, Joe Loth, OSU
Head Coach, Jim Tressel with Lauren

Lou Bonnanzio of the Suffolk County PAL
and Lauren at the inaugural NY 7 on 7
Championship at St. Anthony's High School,
South Huntington, New York

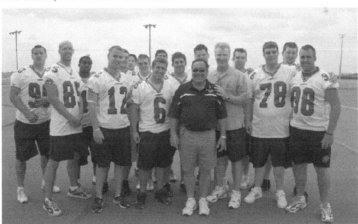

Lafayette College team volunteers with Head Coach,
Frank Tavani and Phil Simms

DEFENSE

Photo by Michael Garner

NOTES

TEAM DEFENSE

Photo by Michael Garner

TEAM DEFENSE DRILLS
Don Dobes, Defensive Coordinator, Dartmouth College

SCREEN DRILL

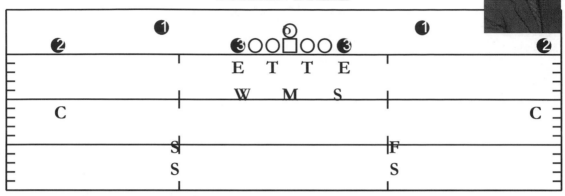

1. All eleven players will align in a defensive call.
2. When the ball is snapped, they will begin to rush or drop according to the call.
3. Six players will be stationed at three different areas on each side of the field simulating (1) a WR screen, (2) a delay screen, (3) or a middle/pop screen. The ball will be thrown to one of these players.
4. Once the ball has been thrown the defense will pursue using correct leverage and communication.

PURSUIT DRILL

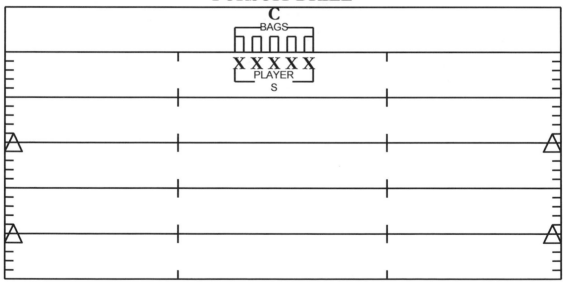

1. 5 players align in front of 5 bags.
2. Coach behind the bag will say go and the 5 players will do 3 up-downs.
3. The coach will point to one side of the field and players will race to a cone on the designated side.
4. The player that doesn't reach a cone will return to the coach to do a predetermined amount of up-downs.
5. Four cones will be used placed ten yards apart.

CHASE TACKLE DRILL

Adam Fuller, Defensive Coordinator, UT - Chattanooga

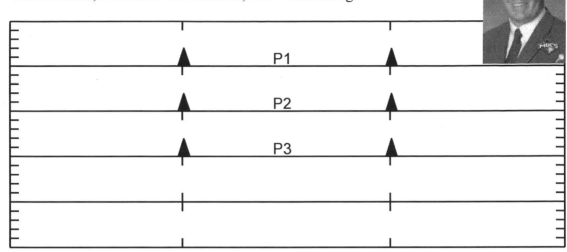

The drill will be setup in a 10 yard box. There will be 3 players involved in the drill, each one aligned at 5 yard increments.

The drill will start with the whistle. The P2 will attempt to score by making a move on P3. P3's goal is to keep P2 out of the end zone which is the line in which the P3 is aligned. The P1 will begin in a chase position and his job is to attack the football from behind; by him being in a chase position it will make the P2 make a decision and go.

Keep score and have a winner.

DEFENSE UNIT PURSUIT DRILLS

Steve Monninger, Defensive Coordinator, Middlebury College

Team Pursuit – Four Cone

Four defensive players will stand evenly spaced in front of coach in a ready position. Coach will give random commands to shuffle in either direction or hit grass for an up-down. When the coach points to a side and yells "Swarm" all four players will run to their cone, placed 5 yards apart, making sure that they do not follow a path of another defender (no tailgating). They will also take the proper angles by going to their proper cone. Drill should be mirrored with two coaches in the middle, so eight players work at one time.

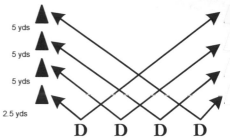

Team Pursuit – Harvard Odd Man Out

Four defensive players will stand evenly spaced in front of coach in a ready position. Coach will give random commands to shuffle in either direction or hit grass for an up-down. When the coach points to a side and yells "Swarm" all four players will run to touch one of the cones placed 5 yards apart. The player who is slowest will not get to touch a cone and go off to the side to do 5 up-downs. Drill should be mirrored with two coaches in the middle, so eight players work at one time.

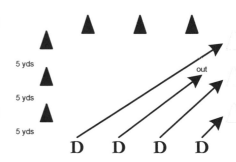

Team Pursuit – Redskin Odd Man Out

Four defensive players will stand evenly spaced in front of coach in a ready position. Players will chop feet in place while coach will give random commands to hit grass for an up-down. When the coach points to a side and yells "Swarm" all four players will run to touch one of the cones placed 5 yards apart. The player who is slowest will not get to touch a cone and go off to the side to do 5 up-downs. Drill should be mirrored with two coaches in the middle, so eight players work at one time.

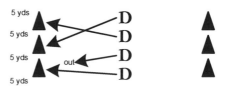

TACKLING DRILLS
Bob Benson, Defensive Coordinator, Colorado School of Mines

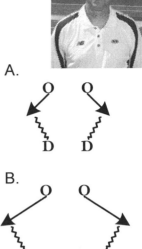

Creep and Tackle

When we have ball carriers we use scout O-linemen and TEs so defensive players are just getting tackling reps.

A. Start 2 yards apart. The Ball Carrier slowly jogs at an angle and the Defender creeps into contact. Start at 1/2 speed and progress to full speed. Make sure they keep posture and creep into a good finish, no lunging.

B. Start 8 yards apart. The Ball Carrier runs and the Defender runs and creeps at the last second 1-2 yards away still gaining ground and finishes the tackle. Progress the drill by giving the ball carrier the ability to cut back and use a stutter step.

Cut, Creep, and Angle Tackle

Same as the drill above, but the defender must first beat a cut block then run, creep and tackle. You can also give the ball carrier the choice to cut back.

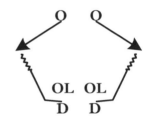

Base Block, Creep, and Angle Tackle

Just like the chop drill, but instead the defender will take on a base block, disengage, run, creep, and, tackle.

QB Aiming Point Tackle

This drill can be done 1 player at a time or with 2.

A. Edge rush keeping our aiming point on the back shoulder of the QB. The Rushers need to take a good path and force the QB to step. The QB should look to spin out or juke and break contain.

B. Inside aiming point. The rushers want to keep their aiming point on the front shoulder of the QB where ever he moves.

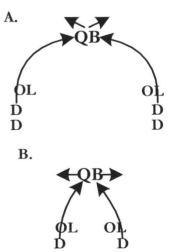

SCREEN PURSUIT

Mark Ross, Head Coach, College of Misericordia

Purpose:

To teach proper pursuit angles vs. bubble screens and rocket screens.

Procedure:

1. A DL, LB, CB and Safety take their alignment vs. a slot set.
2. Form two lines of WR's. The slot WR will run a bubble path 5 yards behind the line. At the same time, the outside WR will take one step up the field then turn back and come straight down the line toward the middle of the field.
3. The drill begins on the Coach's movement. Both WR's will run their route at the same time allowing the Coach to throw to either route.
4. The DL will perform an up down, rush the coach and then take proper pursuit angle to where ball is thrown.
5. The LB will read pass and begin his drop based on the coverage emphasized for the drill.
6. The DB's will take their initial read steps and then break up on ball when it is thrown.
7. All four defenders must pursue to the WR who has caught the ball and fit appropriately based on their leverage.
8. After the first 4 defenders have completed their rep, they exit via the sideline allowing four new defenders to align in their respective positions. Two new WR's will also step up to replace the first two WR's.

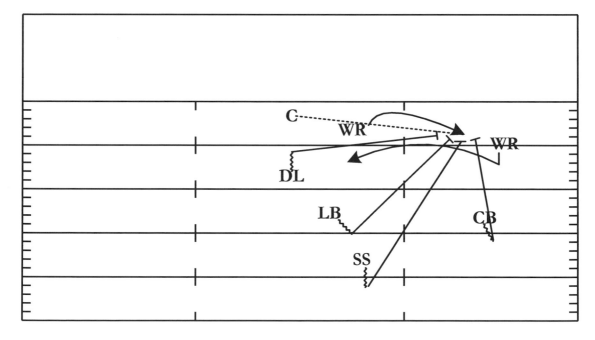

END ZONE PURSUIT DRILL
John Loose, Defensive Coordinator, Lafayette College

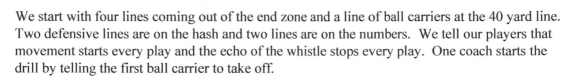

Every spring and every fall this is the first drill we do with our entire defense. It teaches players to run full speed to the ball carrier, proper leverage and coming to football position just prior to contact with the ball carrier. It also teaches proper pursuit angles and can be used as a conditioning drill while still teaching football. Two drills back to back can condition a team of over 100 players in one 8 minute period.

We start with four lines coming out of the end zone and a line of ball carriers at the 40 yard line. Two defensive lines are on the hash and two lines are on the numbers. We tell our players that movement starts every play and the echo of the whistle stops every play. One coach starts the drill by telling the first ball carrier to take off.

We tell the ball carrier to work hard to get outside the defenders and to keep running until the whistle blows. The ball carrier must work back and forth trying to get outside the defenders. The ball carrier must not put his head down and smash his way through the defenders.

The first four defenders will sprint full speed on the ball carrier's movement. The defenders run full speed closing the gap between them and the ball carrier. When they get close all defenders come to balance getting into football position. All four defender will shuffle and squeeze in football position trying to make the ball carrier give ground away from the goal line. Defenders may not grab or push the ball carrier. The drill goes on until the whistle blows or the ball carrier breaks contain and scores. If one defender lets the ball out, the defenders must pick a pursuit angle to get to the ball carrier.

If the ball carrier gets out we make the entire group go again. If the defenders do a great job, they sprint off the field on the whistle and the coach sends the next ball carrier to start the next group. We start out half speed to teach the drill the first time and increase the speed to full once they understand what we are looking for.

We also use the drill with the offensive players. Many play special teams and everyone must be able to pursue, leverage and tackle the ball carrier after a turn over.

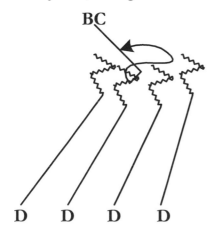
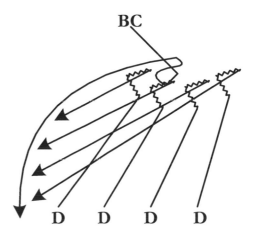

PLANT & GO – FINISH

Larry Kehres, Head Football Coach, Mount Union College & Former AFCA President

<u>Position Drill Related To:</u> Defensive all positions circuit tackling drill

<u>Equipment Needed:</u> 5 Agile Bags

<u>Objectives:</u>
1. To teach and practice the proper technique of executing a tackle.
2. To reinforce the proper football position while incorporating reaction and agility.

<u>Description:</u>
1. Lay four agile bags on the ground spaced out so there is two yards between the middle two bags and one yard between each outside bag and the middle bag.
2. Position a line of tacklers in the middle of the agile bags facing the coach.
3. The coach, holding an agile bag, stands five yards in front of the line of tacklers.
4. On coach's command, the first tackler begins chopping his feet rapidly while maintaining the football position.
5. The coach then points to the right or left to indicate which direction the tackler will break into a lateral shuffle.
6. The tackler will shuffle in the appropriate direction and plant only his outside foot over the end bag and shuffle back in the opposite direction planting only his outside foot over the end bag and shuffle back to the middle where he will burst toward the coach.
7. The coach will extend the agile bag by gripping the handle allowing the tackler to execute a fit tackle on the bag.
8. The drill continues until the whistle blows at which time the tacklers will move to the next station in the tackling circuit.

<u>Coaching Points:</u>
1. Make sure tacklers maintain a good football position as they shuffle laterally through the agile bags.
2. Make sure tacklers do not cross their feet over and that they plant off their outside foot when changing directions.
3. Make sure tacklers use good technique when they fit tackle the bag. Stress exploding the hips, clubbing up with the arms, keeping the head and eyes up.

<u>Safety Considerations:</u>
1. The coach should make sure the ground is level and fairly dry before laying out the agile bags.
2. This drill can be done with full equipment or with no equipment on.

<u>Variations:</u>
1. Incorporate a block protection component by requiring tackler to protect his legs from being reached by a manager throwing an agile bag or rolling a shiver ball at him as he bursts toward the coach.

GOAL LINE PURSUIT
Luke Bussard, Defensive Coordinator, Amherst College

Run Support Drill – "Goal line Pursuit"
We do a drill called "Goal line Pursuit" numerous times each week to practice caging the ball carrier. To do this drill effectively, we will create three lines of defenders, evenly spaced with the middle line directly over the ball carrier and about 40 yards away from a ball carrier [Usually put lines on midline and hash marks].

On the whistle, the ball carrier will sprint toward the defenders straight up field. The defenders will be doing the same, closing on the ball carrier as fast as possible. As the gap between the two decreases, the defenders must sink their hips and "come to balance" in a good football position. As the ball carrier chooses a direction, the defender outside of him in the direction the ball carrier runs, becomes the *Force Player*. The defender in the middle is the *Cutback Player* and the outside defender away from him is the *Fence Player*.

There are key coaching points to each position. The *Force Player* must always keep his outside leg back so that he does not "box" his hips, potentially allowing the back outside. His job is to force the ball back to the *Cutback Player* who will remain in the back hip of the ball carrier. The *Fence Player* must take an angle of about 5 yards down field so that he can position himself to make a play if the ball carrier is able to get outside of the *Force Player*.

When the ball carrier changes directions, the jobs of the *Fence Player* and the *Force Player* switch. Now the *Fence Player* must change directions and cutoff the ball carrier, becoming the *Force Player*. The *Force Player* must now change directions and take a proper path of pursuit as the new *Fence Player*. The job of the *Cutback Player* does not change, he must flip his hips and remain in the back hip of the ball carrier.

When we do this drill, we never allow the players to use their hands. They must use their feet to get into position to make a play. Note: Works best if ball carrier "travels" a few yards [5] prior to changing direction.

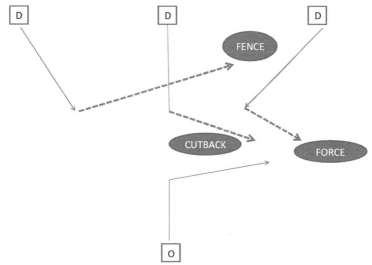

BOX TACKLE

Mark Reardon, Defensive Coordinator, Villanova University

Equipment:
4 Cones, 2 Footballs

Objective:
To teach and practice the proper techniques and fundamentals of tackling in the open field.

Description:
1. Place 4 cones ten yards apart in the shape of a box. (See diagram)
2. Position a line of players on each side of the box. One group will serve as the tacklers and one as the ball carrier.
3. The coach will position himself on one side of the box. He will initiate the drill with a whistle or clap.
4. On the coaches command the ball carrier and tackler will move toward one another. The objective of the ball carrier is to make the tackler miss through a series of cuts within the box. (Limit to 2 or 3)
5. The tackler must engage the ball carrier using the proper technique.
6. The drill should continue until all tacklers have had sufficient work.

Coaching Points:
1. The tacklers should be instructed to maintain proper balance and leverage on the ball carrier.
2. Instruct tacklers about vision on the belly button of the ball carrier and not over striding into the tackle.
3. Instruct the tacklers on the specific elements when tackling. Such as foot fire, hip explosion and head placement.

Safety Considerations:
1. It is imperative to warm up before all drill work.
2. All personnel should be instructed as to the proper fundamentals prior to initiating the drill.
3. The drill should progress from form to live tackling.
4. The coach should monitor closely the intensity of the drill.

Variations:
1. Can be used as form or live tackle.
2. The drill perimeters can be narrowed or expanded based upon emphasis.
3. A block can be incorporated in the drill.

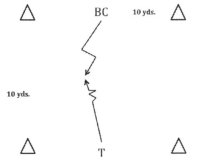

UCONN TEAM TACKLING DRILL

Hank Hughes, Assistant Head Coach, University of Connecticut

Angle Tackle:

- Defender will work to properly fit up tackle between the cones
- Start 5 yards from bag and start on coach's command
- Ball Carrier attempt to make defender miss and get through the cones
- Defender will secure tackle and drive the ball carrier back

Coaching Points:

- Gain ground and take away cutback
- Focus on near breastplate
- Take ball carrier on an angle
- Run feet through tackle
- Rip up and grab cloth

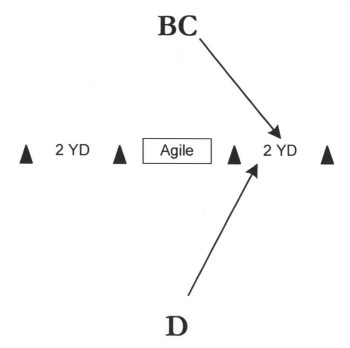

TEAM PURSUIT

John Loose, Defensive Coordinator, Lafayette College

Every day at Lafayette College we grade our players on effort. We teach them commitment when it comes to effort and each other. When the ball is away, you either turn and look or turn and run. Each time a player doesn't run full speed to the ball through the echo of the whistle we give the defense one lack of effort (LOE). That gives the defense eleven possible LOE's on each and every play. The players are graded during every full team 11 on 11 and 7 on 7 pass periods. Every day we run the following pursuit drill one time for every LOE from the previous practice. Our kids learn very fast how important it is to give relentless effort on every play. The veterans will push the young players so they don't have to run pursuits all day.

To emphasize the importance of turnovers we reward them by giving them back five LOEs for each turnover. In addition we give back three for each sack, but only in scrimmage situations when we can get a more accurate count on what would actually be a sack if it were a game.

We start by having two or three defensive huddles on the sideline. Two Running Backs are used behind the QB played by the defensive coordinator. A receiver is also placed on line of scrimmage (LOS) at each end. We use our kickers as RBs and WRs. We place a coach behind the LOS on both sides and one in the middle to monitor the drill (Diagram 1).

We do not use a ball for the initial drill. The coordinator signals the first group to take the field. The entire huddle must sprint full speed and set the huddle in front of the coordinator. As they are taking the field the coach will give them a huddle call. As they break the huddle the coach will give personnel grouping and formation. The coach can trade, shift or motion the set. The first huddle must be responsible the first day for every possible huddle call and offensive formation. The second huddle is more basic and if we have a third huddle it is kept even more basic. An entire game plan can be practiced this way. It is a fast pace drill that demands concentration, communication and effort. The coach running the drill acts as the QB. He moves the drill around, changing field position from hash to middle back to the hash.

After any formation adjustments the coordinator signals a snap followed by a toss sweep or drop back pass with a motion to one of the receivers. If it is toss action, the RB runs a toss sweep course and keeps going up the sideline (Diagram 2). If it is a pass action the receiver fakes a catch and proceeds up the sideline. The backs can go full speed, but the receivers must take time to make the fake catch and run at ¾ speed to time up the drill for the entire defense (Diagram 3).

The defense must execute the call then pursue the ball full speed taking the proper angle to the ball. Every player must touch the ball carrier with two hands below the waist while in football position (FBP). Defenders may not grab or push the ball carrier at any time. After touching the ball carrier, each defender turns to the coach behind the LOS to the side of the ball carrier. The defenders run their feet in FBP and do up downs on the coach's command. The coach will then call the entire defense to him for a break down. The players sprint full speed and break down around the coach still moving their feet in FBP. We constantly coach our players to start and finish every play in FBP. We want knee benders, not waist benders (Diagram 4). After the break down, the defense sprints off the field to the nearest sideline.

TEAM PURSUIT

John Loose, Defensive Coordinator, Lafayette College

If the adjustments and defense are not executed properly the entire group will go again. If the effort, leverage or FBP are not performed correctly the entire group goes again. If it is done correctly the next group takes the field and the drill continues. Once the basic concept of the drill is understood, fumble recoveries, interceptions returns, different screen pursuits, pass actions, cutback pursuits and even red zone can be added to the drill.

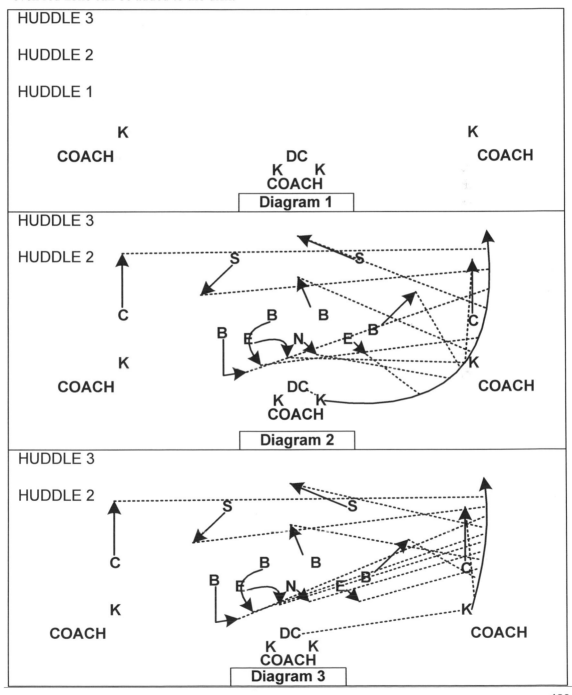

PASS PURSUIT DRILL

Dave Cohen, Defensive Coordinator, Western Michigan University

The purpose of the drill is to teach the proper reactions of the defense once a ball is intercepted.

The offensive players needed for the drill are three receivers and a quarterback. The receivers are fifteen yards from the line of scrimmage. Receiver 1 is halfway between the right sideline and hash, the middle receiver is half way between the hash marks and receiver 3 is halfway between the left hash and left sideline.

The drill begins on the goal line upon the quarterbacks ball movement. On ball movement the defensive front does an up-down to clear the quarterbacks throwing lane. The coverage players take a zone drop for the called coverage. The quarterback will throw the ball in the direction of one of the receivers. The closest defender to the ball will intercept the ball. The next closest defender to the intended receiver will block him as he is the most common tackler of an interceptor. The defensive front will pursue to the intended receiver, once they see it is an interception they will find the quarterback and block him as he is the second most common tackler of the interceptor. The remaining defenders will escort the interceptor past the goal line in a wall like fashion looking to make a legal above the waist block.

The drill will end when the wall escort and interceptor all cross the goal line.

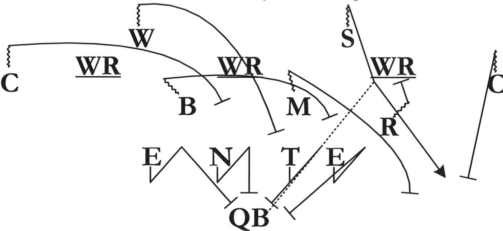

½ LINE ROUTE COMBOS

Doug McFadden, Defensive Backs Coach, Lafayette College

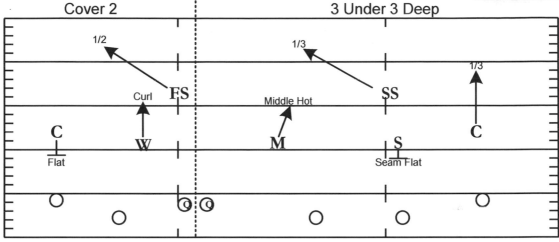

Purpose:

This is a realistic drill where your guys are able to see and fill where their help is within a zone coverage. We are able to run through all route combos vs. all of our coverages.

Coaching Points:

- Concentrate on keys, drops, and communication.
- Move ball from hash to middle of field to hash.
- Change between 1 to 3 WRs on each side and even use backs out of the backfield.
- Have one side go while you give the other side routes and coverage. Get as many reps as possible while having your scout WRs rotate in as needed.

NOTES

DEFENSIVE LINE

Photo by Michael Garner

DEFENSIVE LINE PASS RUSH DRILLS

Greg Bryant, Defensive Line Coach, Fort Hayes State University

Pass Rush Set & Corner:

Equipment:
6 Cones, 2 Hand Shields & Pop-Up

Objective:
To teach DL proper use of knocking OL hands & getting to corner. Also teaches get off & proper body lean around the corner.

Description:
Break off into two lines - E & N - T & R, align them behind a yard line. Align cones - on yard line & 4 yards away & one at 7 yards. Coach aligns on LOS & gives cadence, snaps ball or provides movement. DL explodes forward on snap &sprints to cone at 4 dips underneath cone at 7 yards. Man at 4-yard cone shoots hands at DL to simulate OL pass set. DL knocks down OL hands while sprinting to 7 yard cone.

Coaching Points:
1. DL must explode out of stance & stay on hard line to cone.
2. DL must gain ground on first step, claw grass, step forward with same foot.
3. DL must anticipate OL hands, be ready and quick with swat and rip, continue accelerating.
4. Lean shoulder into turn & burst underneath 7 yard cone.
5. Finish through cone - through the QB.

Pass Rush Pop Up Gauntlet:

Equipment:
4 Pop Ups or 4 Hand Shields

Objective:
To teach DL how to open hips & maneuver in tight spaces against an OL pass set. Also teaches arm movements and agility.

Description:
Four DL align on 5 yard increments in a straight in a straight line, with the last man aligned at an angle away from last man. DL aligns in front of 1st man. Coach aligns in front of DL with ball. On snap DL explodes to first man & works a slap rip on DL. DL continues through bags slaloming on both sides of the bags, R & L. The DL works a spin on the last man and bursts through the cone.

Coaching Points:
1. DL must open hips when slapping & ripping.
2. Feet must be constantly moving along with hands.
3. Speed through drill is essential.
4. Players should keep good body lean & burst through men as tight as possible.
5. Eyes must be up, see where you rush.
6 DL must get hips open on each bag.

DEFENSIVE LINE PASS RUSH DRILLS

Greg Bryant, Defensive Line Coach, Fort Hayes State University

Pass Rush Cloth Drill:

Objective:
To teach DL proper escape around OL during pass rush.

Description:
The DL partner up & face each other across a yard line. One side of line is DL, the other side is OL. Coach stands behind the DL to watch technique. On command, DL gets into a football position with feet buzzing. Coach then gives another command & DL snatches OL outside shoulder with their outside arm & opens hips. After controlling shoulder of OL, the DL should jerk shoulder down, & perform rip move. DL must burst after controlling shoulder & while using rip move. The DL resets and goes on coaches command. The player should get 4 reps before switching over to the arm.

Coaching Points:
1. DL must open hips when snatching shoulder of OL & extend arm fully.
2. Rip move must be performed at full speed & must jerk shoulder down with violence.
3. Teaches DL to get skinny when opening hips.
4. Once control of shoulder is obtained, rip move & acceleration must be emphasized to get QB.
5. Make sure pads are down & knees are bent throughout the drill.

ROOHAH'S

Antoine Smith, Defensive Line, College of the Holy Cross

Objective:

- For the defender to explode off the ground
- React to the command
- Pursuit to the landmark (cone)

Coaching Points:

- Eyes on the Offender
- Maintain low pad level
- Sprint outside of drill with 4 seconds in between groups
- Seat Rolls, left, right, chest down, point to a cone, all defenders on a dead sprint there

Tempo:

- High Tempo
- 2 Reps per group
- All 3 or 4 depending on your front, breakdown with a clap

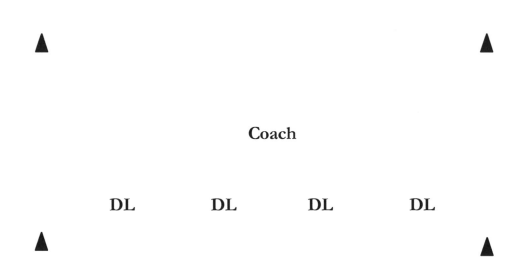

REACTION TO MOVEMENT

Mark Fetterman, Defensive Line Coach, Widener University

Objectives:

Teach proper rush stance
Teach proper takeoff
Teach reaction to pass; pull; screen; draw
Work both right hand and left hand stance

Procedure:

Check rush stance
Move on coach's movement
Explode out of stance
Replace hand on 1st step
Sprint and react to coach's movement
Defensive man goes to OL; repeat

Coaching Points:

Make sure proper hand is down
Gain ground on every step
Sink hips on COD

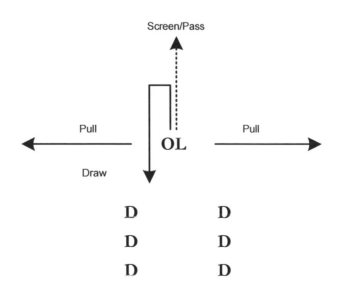

DEFENSIVE LINE DRILLS

Ian Dell, Defensive Line Coach, Moravian College

Defensive Line – Single Block Reaction Drill:

Allow me to start off by saying that this drill is very versatile. Usually we build up to this drill by using only one of the blocking techniques, mentioned later, for each of the three repetitions and then gradually incorporate new blocks as the season progresses. Also, depending on the skill level of the athlete, we may only take the first couple steps of the rep to begin with, and then incorporate an escape technique later on. There are also various things you can do at the end of the drill to incorporate other skills, such as scoop and score or a form tackle. Because of the versatility and multiple skills used in this drill, the drill is valuable for time restricted practices.

The drill is run as follows; keeping in mind you can change the format to meet your specific needs: using scout offensive lineman, align three players about five yards apart on the line of scrimmage. Each scout lineman will be assigned blocking technique pre-drill without letting the defensive lineman know that technique. The defensive player aligns, head up or in a shade, on the first offensive lineman. The first offensive lineman begins the drill on his movement, performing either a base block, cut block or reach block. The defensive lineman reacts to the block of the offensive lineman and performs the necessary technique to maintain his gap control. Immediately after execution of the first repetition, the defensive lineman moves down the line to the second offensive lineman and this is repeated, followed by a third repetition on the third offensive lineman.

Techniques:

In defeating these three blocks the focus on technique will be as follows: coaches are looking for low pad level and square shoulders at all times. Coming out of the stance there needs to be good forward lean and a flat back. Also, it is essential to maintain a wide base to remain balanced and react as athletically as possible. The defensive lineman should attack the block with an explosive first step of about six inches, and react to the block at this point. If the focus is on hands coming out of their stance, as opposed to the feet, you will see that the feet follow naturally. In the past this focus has helped keep pad levels low in our younger players. At no point should any defensive lineman catch a block. It is important that the first step gets down as quickly as possible to be able to react to the block. The reaction to the block will be based off the movement of the hand targets.

Base block:

If a base block is performed by the offensive lineman, the technique to be focused on is shooting the inside hand to the breast plate, and the gap hand to the shoulder cuff closest to the assigned gap. As stated before, we want to focus on shooting our hands to our target, and allow the feet to naturally follow. On contact we are grabbing cloth so we can control the blocker. We are emphasizing a strong punch and placement with the hands, low pad level, a wide base, as well as short driving steps. From here we work to extend our arms and create lift on the blocker. This will allow us to create leverage on the offensive lineman, and put ourselves in a more powerful body position. While maintaining leverage to the assigned gap, the defensive lineman must create backward movement on the offensive lineman. Here it is important that our steps remain short and explosive, and that we maintain extension with our arms. Arm extension and separation will also allow us to keep the shoulder cuff hand in a position that the defensive lineman can use it to escape and make a play in his gap.

DEFENSIVE LINE DRILLS
Ian Dell, Defensive Line Coach, Moravian College

Reach Block:

Similar to the base block, hand placement is essential to defeating the reach block and maintaining gap control. At the point of recognition of a reach block, the hands should shoot to the breast plate and shoulder cuff nearest the gap, and grab cloth. With the breast plate hand, the defensive lineman should pull the offensive lineman toward their body and push up field with the hand on the shoulder cuff until he reestablishes body position in his assigned gap. Steps should be up field as much as possible, but lateral to the point of regaining gap leverage. From here, he can escape the block to the gap responsibility. It is imperative that the shoulders remain square and the feet are used to get the body in the correct position. If the shoulders get turned, the defensive lineman has essentially removed himself from the play and the gaps become bigger.

Cut Block:

Again hand placement is important. At the point of recognition of the cut block the defensive lineman must redirect his hand targets slightly. The defensive lineman must stop the momentum of the offensive lineman by punching the hands to the back of the helmet and the top of the shoulder pad nearest his body. While doing so, the hips need to be thrown into the gap and ground must be given with the feet to maintain separation from the offensive lineman. It is critical to maintain gap control and not allow the offensive lineman to get into his legs or cut him off from gap responsibility. As mentioned before, he is not catching this block. After the quick first step react to the block and defeat it while staying on balance and in an athletic stance, ready to make a play on the ball carrier.

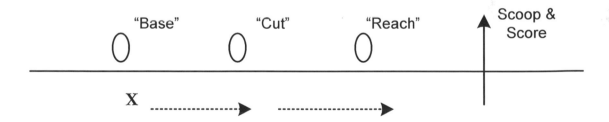

DEFENSIVE LINE TAKE-OFF AND BLOCK RECOGNITION

Ethan Jeros, Defensive Line Coach, William Paterson University

Take Off = "Create a TRAIN WRECK"

      PRIORITY

1. Attack the LOS. creating a new one
   a. Head- "V" of the neck- Hairline under the chin.
   b. Hands- On the breastplate, grabbing cloth, thumbs at 1:00 & 11:00.
      Vs. Run- Control man, then escape.
      Vs. Pass- Keep OL's hands off.
   c. Feet- Power Step/Slide Step (Step with back foot first).
   d. Hands and feet NEVER stop moving (Always be active).

- Snap your hips underneath you.
- Run/Excite your feet; "Walk OL back".
- Read your keys.
- Explosion.
- Pads stay SQUARE, unless on a movement.
- Hands at eye level or higher.
- Strike a blow on the rise and with violence.
- All movement is up field and blows should be delivered with quickness.
- Always "Excite" or "Chatter" the feet. Do not let your feet die.
- Redirect/Retrace at full speed.
- Keep hands inside of feet and elbows inside of hips.

Block Recognition:

As a defensive lineman, there are basic blocks that you will receive and you must understand how to take them on. As the season progresses and the team gets into specific schemes, these basic fundamental reminders will help as you get into more complex blocking patterns by diverse offenses.

1. **Base Block:** When the OL you are aligned on blocks you straight up. Defeating the base block, you must beat him off the ball with your hands and feet, while your pad level is lower than his. Always maintain your gap integrity and stay square maintaining your gap integrity!

2. **Reach Block:** When the OL you are aligned on tries to get outside of your gap and overtake you. Defeating the reach block, you must take a hard up field charge and recognize his "V" of the neck is attempting to gain leverage on you. Make sure to lock your outside arm on the outside shoulder of the OL, while pulling with your inside arm and keeping your feet excited. Maintaining square shoulders is imperative. Once you beat the man, you will release as stated earlier. You are never reached until you are reached, meaning, he may beat you initially, but you are not beat unless he turns his shoulders. That is why you must press his outside shoulder and beat his leverage!

3. **Cutoff Block:** When the OL you are aligned on tries to get inside of you when the play is away. This block is similar to a Down block, meaning, the OL is taking an inside release, so your immediate reaction must be to squeeze his outside shoulder and move towards the LOS laterally, not trying to get too far up field. As always, stay square, but do not get too far up field, as this will open up holes for the RB and if a puller is coming back at you, will make it easier for him to create lanes.

DL POP UP BAG DRILLS

Tony Thompson, Defensive Line Coach, Stony Brook University

Use Pop Up Bags – usually 5 or 6. Bags 2 feet apart. Good for conditioning.
Concentrate on footwork or on hand quickness or on hips.

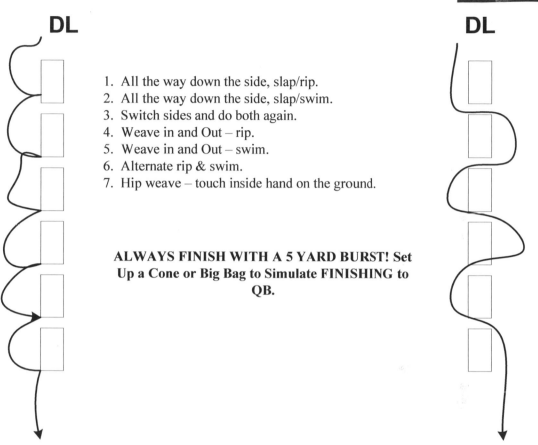

DL

1. All the way down the side, slap/rip.
2. All the way down the side, slap/swim.
3. Switch sides and do both again.
4. Weave in and Out – rip.
5. Weave in and Out – swim.
6. Alternate rip & swim.
7. Hip weave – touch inside hand on the ground.

ALWAYS FINISH WITH A 5 YARD BURST! Set Up a Cone or Big Bag to Simulate FINISHING to QB.

DL

Big Bag Circuit:

Start DL in a stance to work on take off. At the first bag execute a club-rip, then a club-swim at the second bag. The third bag needs to be tilted and the DL must dip his shoulder under for a rip movement. On the last bag the DL must flip his hips as the bag is tilted at him by the coach. Once he clears the bag he sprints to the man holding the shield and executes a bull rush.

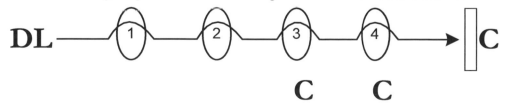

DOUBLE TEAM DRILL

Joe Dougherty, Defensive Line Coach, Lafayette College

Set-up:

The diagram represents a 5-man sled. The X's will simulate Offensive Linemen blocking on a double team. The X's are players holding hand shields. The D's are the defensive lineman.

1. The defensive linemen are in their stances, in front of the end pad of the 5-man sled.

2. The defensive linemen fire out of their stances and engage the sled as they would an offensive lineman. Coaching points are wide base and leg drive. They should be driving the sled, not pushing w/out leg movement. They should be running through the sled.

3. Once the defensive linemen initiate contact w/ the sled, the players holding the pads step out and press the hand shields against the defensive linemen's hip, simulating a double team.

4. At Lafayette we teach the defensive linemen to honor the 2nd blocker by fighting pressure with their hips and not getting knocked off. We teach to split double teams by collapsing the offensive lineman we are aligned over.

5. The coaching point should be to have the defensive linemen drive their feet while honoring the pressure of the second blocker.

**** In the interest of safety make sure that the "blockers" hit the defensive linemen ONLY on their hips. DO NOT put pressure on the defensive linemen's elbows or arms.

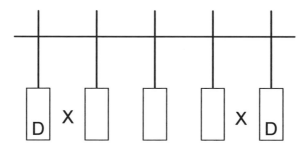

DEFENSIVE LINE CHANGE OF DIRECTION DRILL

Mickey Rehring, Defensive Line Coach, Bowdoin College

Have each player start in a two-point stance on either side of the top 3 bags of the square. With low pad level, have the athlete shuffle through the top of the square while facing toward the cones. Once both feet are outside the 3rd bag, they must accelerate and run over the next two bags. From there, they must sink their hips and shuffle over another bag before running full speed at the middle cone. A coach should be situated at the middle cone and give the athlete a direction to run through the final cone. First time through, make it known which cone they will finish through. After each athlete has done the drill known in both directions, then the coach may direct players to either final cone.

Coaching Points:

- Athletes must always face toward the cones.
- Make sure of great, low pad level throughout the drill.
- When attacking the middle cone, make sure each athlete accelerates towards it, forcing him to react from a full sprint.
- To finish, the athlete must run directly over the final cone forcing him to run a flat, straight line to the cone and not bending his finish.
- May also incorporate a "scoop & score" aspect as they run through the final cone to get extra awareness from the athlete and more turn-over work.

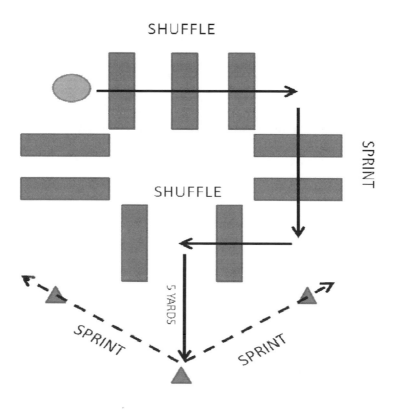

CHOP/CLUB/RIP-OVERSET HOOP DRILL

Mike Saint Germain, Defensive Line Coach, Franklin & Marshall College

Normal Set by OL- Chop/Rip by the DL outside of the OL and lean as you get around the hoop to QB finish.

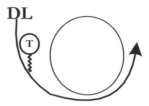

Overset by OL- Club/Rip by the DL inside of the OL, lean back to not get washed down and lean as you get past the hip of OL and lean to the QB finish.

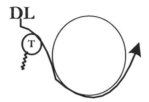

Coaching Points:
- Ball get off is essential.
- Reacting to the overset and planting off the outside foot and coming back under is important.
- When working against a normal set, a hard chop/rip and good lean is necessary.
- Have players exaggerate lean by grabbing grass around hoop on way to the finish.

Kneeling Fit Starts:
- DL will start in a fit position while kneeling, hands in a good fit position, depending on whether you want him head up or shaded to either side on the OL.
- On command the DL will press the OL with his hands and get his foot on the leg that is kneeling into the ground as fast as he physically can.
- From that point the DL will run his feet and drive the OL, with short choppy steps.
- After 3 yards the DL can rip off the OL to either side as directed.
- Biggest points of emphasis for this drill; getting that first foot into the ground as quickly as possible, pressing with your hands, and getting your feet into the ground as quickly as possible with your steps.

Stance/Drive in Chute:
- Start the DL and OL in the chute a ball's distance away from one another and half way into the chute.
- You can start the DL head up or shaded to either side of the OL, at the snap of the ball you want the DL to strike with his hands and step with the foot that is back.
- Unless we are moving, we want the hand that is down to strike the V of the neck on the OL and the hand that is up strike his armpit; press on contact with both hands.
- The foot that is back will take a 6 inch step. Short choppy steps will continue after the first foot strike.
- From that sequence with his ball get off, hands and feet, the DL will drive the OL out of the chute.
- Major coaching points are hand placement, foot height and frequency of steps, play with your eyes behind your hands and keeping low pad level throughout the duration of the drill.

PASS, DRAW, SCREEN DRILL
Nick Bach, Defensive Line Coach, East Stroudsburg University

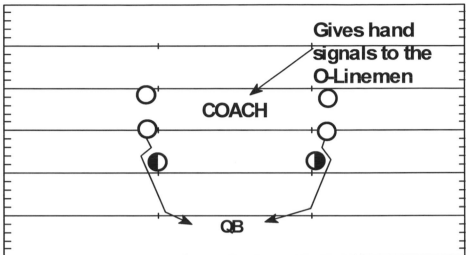

This drill is designed to train defensive linemen to react to these specific plays. Each defensive lineman will line up in an outside shade on the offensive lineman. A coach or player will be the QB. The other coach will stand behind the defensive line and will signal to the offensive line whether they should block like it is a pass, draw, or screen. Defensive linemen should always begin by yelling "PASS!", since all of these blocks appear to be the same at first.

Screen – If OL releases down the field, DL should react to screen by grabbing cloth and retracting steps.

Draw – If OL opens the gate and pushes the DL outside and up field, DL should react to draw by squeezing L inside and ripping across his face.

Pass – If QB passes, DL's should hit a pass rush move and pursue their proper QB pursuit angle or "Quadrant".

Note – QB can scramble or sprint out to make drill more realistic (I let players rotate at QB so they can have some fun trying to make each other miss).

NOTES

LINEBACKERS

ALLEY DRILL

Dave Steckel, Defensive Coordinator, University of Missouri

Purpose:

The Alley Drill develops the player's ability to read and react versus the ball carrier's movement.

Equipment / Set-up:

Two footballs. Two lines of players on a side line, set to run across the field, separated by ten yards.

Instructions:

The drill will begin off of the "offensive" player running straight across the field to the near hash marks. In his course he will change speeds multiple times. The defensive player will mirror the offensive player to keep a good cut-back relationship, closing in front of the ball carrier before reaching the finish. By the end of the offensive player's course the defender should finish in front of the offensive player.

Key Points:

The coach wants to make sure the player is not taking a false step in his initial movement. The defender must keep his shoulders parallel to the line of scrimmage and shuffle down the line while closing in on the offensive player. When the offensive player changes speed, the defender needs to change speed. To keep the relationship, a cross step and run movement may be needed. The defender should stay in the offensive player's back pocket to ensure no cut-backs.

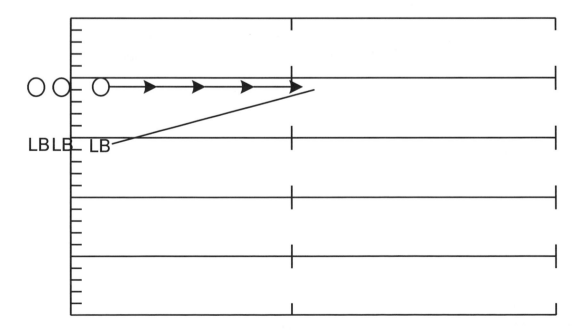

MACHINE GUN DRILL

Paul Darragh, Defensive Coordinator, Bloomsburg University

At Bloomsburg University we stress the importance of defeating blocks and attacking the football. We use many drills to improve our ability to escape the different types of blocks we see and to "Finish" with a great tackle. The main coaching points in these drills are consistent with great defense: Good pad level, aggressive mentality, use of hands, and always "Finish".

Skill:

Defeating multiple blocks (high/low) with a finishing tackle

Blockers 3 yards apart, staggered

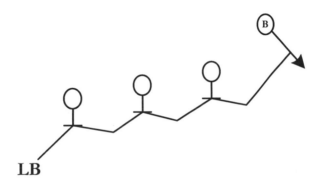

Coach: signal to blockers high or low block

Note: Initially we introduce this drill with one blocker and progress to three

COUNTER DRILL

Keith Migliorino, Defensive Coordinator, Kean University

Purpose:

This drill will help your LB's play the counter effectively. The counter is one of the more difficult running plays in football to defend. This drill will teach a linebacker how to effectively change direction once he recognizes the play is a counter.

Description:

Set up 3 cones, the first two will be 2 yards apart, the third will be 4 yards from those 2 (3 cones in a straight line, 6 yards long, see diagram below). The player should be in a good two point stance, 3 yards deep straddling the middle cone. On the coaches command the LB will take 1 or 2 short shuffles to the cone that is nearest to him. When he reaches that cone he will react as if he has seen counter. The LB will then change direction, begin a crossover run accelerating around the farthest cone.

Coaching Points:

The coaching points for the short shuffle is to keep the shoulders square and do not cross your feet. Do not HOP while shuffling. Keep your body level. For the crossover run, stay square to the line of scrimmage and the player should kick his heel out toward the direction he is moving. This will force the LB's hips and shoulders to stay square. While accelerating around the farthest cone, stay square to the line of scrimmage.

Equipment:

3 cones

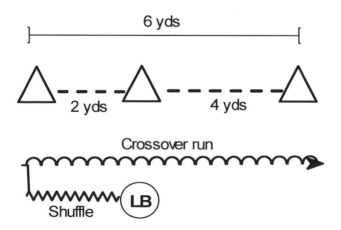

MIRROR DRILL

Keith Migliorino, Defensive Coordinator, Kean University

Purpose:

The purpose of this drill is to teach linebackers how to keep inside leverage on a running back on any outside run (toss, pitch, outside zone option, etc.). It emphasizes not over playing a running back in case of a cut back. It also teaches linebackers to shuffle without crossing their feet and staying square to the line of scrimmage. Another important aspect of this drill is the crossover run, which is used when the ball carrier picks up speed. Both the shuffle and the cross over run will be utilized in game situations.

Description:

Set up 5 cones 10 yards apart. There are two lines of players on either side of the cone. One line being the ball carrier and the other being the linebacker. The running back starts out in a slow jog, the linebacker (5 yards away) will shuffle "mirroring" the ball carrier. The LB must keep inside *leverage* on the running back, by always keeping his outside shoulder on the backside hip of the RB. The objective is to not overplay the RB. When the ball carrier hits the second cone he will begin a 3/4 sprint, which will force the linebacker to begin a cross over run, enabling him to keep inside leverage. When the ball carrier reaches the third cone he will then gear down to a slow jog, which forces the linebacker to get back into a slow shuffle, continuing to keep inside leverage on the ball carrier. Finally at the fourth cone the ball carrier returns to a 3/4 sprint and the LB mirrors him with a crossover run. The drill ends with both the RB and LB meeting on a 45 degree angle with a form tackle.

Coaching Points:

The coaching points for the shuffle is to keep shoulders square to the ball carrier or line of scrimmage and to not your cross feet. It is very important that the linebacker NOT hop while shuffling. For the crossover run, the player needs to stay square to line of scrimmage and kick his heel out toward the direction he is moving. This will force the LB's hips and shoulders to stay square. To maintain inside leverage, the LB must keep the ball carrier on his outside shoulder at all times.

Equipment:

5 cones and a football

LINEBACKER TACKLING DRILLS

Paul Dean, Head Football Coach, Ohio Northern University

(A) Form Tackle Drill:

2 bags facing each other long ways. RB and LB at each end facing each other. RB takes step to one side of bag and runs while the LB form tackles him.

(B) Angle Tackle Drill:

4 bags put together making a cross sign. RB runs outside of bag on an angle. LB angle tackles him.

(C) Open Field Tackle Drill:

2 bags facing each other long ways. RB and LB face each other 5 yards from the bags. RB takes step to one side of bag and runs to the bag, then breaks either right or left. LB should work toward the RB reeling in the slack and keeping the RB inside and in front of him

(D) Sideline Tackle Drill:

RB and LB face each other behind cones. RB runs toward the sideline outside of the cone. The LB   shuffles toward the RB staying on the backside hip of the RB squeezing him to the sideline. (Use the sideline as an extra defender)

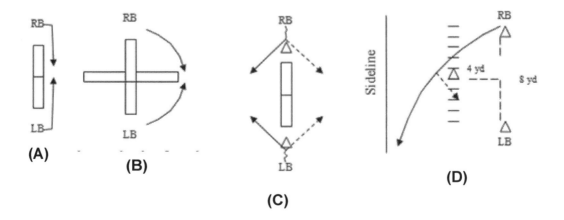

BLOCK DESTRUCTION
Luke Thompson, Linebackers Coach, Georgetown University

3-MAN SLED DRILL:

Emphasis on defeating blockers trying to reach you or cut you off at the 2nd level

1. Set LBs up at 45 degree angle from end bag
2. On coach's movement, LB will attack bag at 45 degree angle and strike with two hands
3. LB will lock arms out and find ball to outside of bag
4. LB will rip off bag and finish vertical as close to the sled as possible

Coaching Points:

1. LB must play at 45 degree angle
2. Strike bag with thumbs up in order to control OL
3. Separate from bag and find ball to outside with feet chopping
4. Violently club and rip off bag while still staying as tight to sled as possible (keep angle on ball carrier)

5-MAN SLED DRILL:

Emphasis on block destruction with various uses of the hands

1. LB will start at 1st bag of sled
2. On coach's movement, LB strikes 1st bag with thumbs up
3. After initial strike, LB shuffles to 3rd bag where he executes a wipe move on bag
4. LB shuffles to 5th bag where he clubs and rips violently to outside while staying as tight to sled as possible

Coaching Points:

1. Play low
2. Violent with hands
3. Finish tight to final bag

TWO-MAN DIVE AND CUTBACK DRILL

Chris Sprague, Linebackers Coach, Lock Haven University

The purpose of this drill is to have the linebackers learn to play off various types of blocks and make a tackle. In addition, this drill will give the linebackers an idea of how the backside will flow and fit up with a play that may cutback.

Two bags are laid on the ground parallel to each other approximately 8 yards apart. Two offensive lineman are positioned between the bags approximately two yards apart, with a ball carrier about five yards behind them. The linebackers will align with their heels at 4 yards, facing the offensive linemen.

The coach signals to the blockers to drive block, reach or low block to either side of the linebackers, the ball carrier will run to the "point of attack". The ball carrier will have a two way go, outside the offensive lineman and inside the bag or cutback to the middle. The linebackers will play off the blocks and fit into their proper "window" and make the tackle.

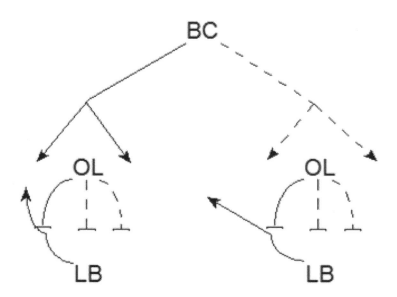

BLUFFTON LINEBACKER DRILLS

Tyson Veidt, Head Coach, Bluffton University

Edge Rush Drill:

1. Begin in edge rush stance with outside foot back, square to LOS, toes up field, weight on up field foot.
2. Key the ball for take-off sprint by first bag.
3. Use a rip move and bend tight around second dummy and under QB spot and finish through the second dot.
4. Transition through the drill without hesitation.

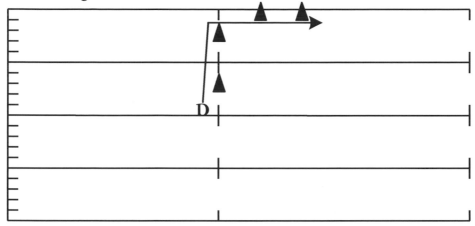

Combination Bag Drill:

1. Begin in good stance.
2. First movement is to weave through bags.
3. Second movement is to shuffle over the bags.
4. Third movement is to defeat chop block and butt the top of each bag.
5. The fourth movement is to burst out and finish through the cones.
6. Focus on keeping hips down and back, shoulders down, stay square with pads and use your hands across the top.

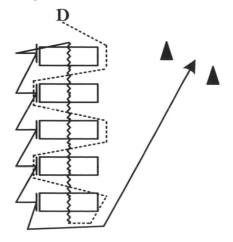

TRANSITION & LEVERAGE DRILLS

Lew Acquarulo, Defensive Coordinator, Trinity College

Drill Name: Lead, Scrape and Plug (1)

Objective: Train the LB in the fundamental movements of the position.

Procedure: Drill will be performed from the sideline toward the hash marks. The coach will stand on the sideline facing into the field. The LB will Lead Step in the direction of flow given by the Coach. The LB scrapes to the cone and tightly plugs to the trash can. The LB must break down into a good form tackle position with the proper leverage, given by the Coach, on the can.

Coaching Points:

Lead Step: Be sure LB pushes off back foot in direction of flow. Coach should simulate Power Flow.

Scrape : LB should fight to stay square. At cone, LB should point inside foot up field in direction of can.

Leverage Tackle : LB's feet should become choppy and widen with proper leverage on can.

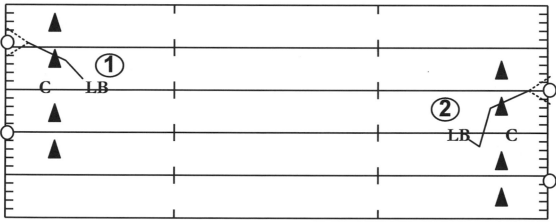

Drill Name: Lead, Redirect, Scrape and Plug (2)

Objective: Train the LB in the fundamental movements of the position.

Coaching Points:

Lead Step: Coach should simulate Power Flow. Be sure LB pushes off back foot in direction of flow and maintains weight on inside half of foot. Coach should then simulate conflict. LB should redirect within one step of recognizing the puller.

Scrape: LB should fight to stay square. At cone, LB should point inside foot up field in direction of can.

Leverage Tackle : LB's feet should become choppy and widen with proper leverage on can.

TRANSITION & LEVERAGE DRILLS

Lew Acquarulo, Defensive Coordinator, Trinity College

Drill Name: Lead, Crossover and Plug (1)

Objective: Train the LB in the fundamental movements of the position.

Coaching Points:

Lead Step: Coach should simulate Fast Flow. Be sure LB pushes off back foot in direction of flow and maintains weight on inside half of foot.

Scrape : LB should crossover run and fight to stay square. At cone, LB should point inside foot up field in direction of can.

Leverage Tackle : LB's feet should become choppy and widen with proper leverage on can.

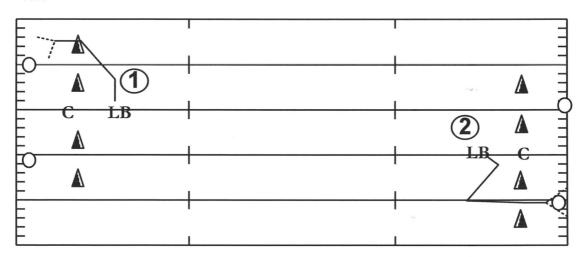

Drill Name: Lead, 45 Degrees, and Transition (2)

Objective: Train the LB in the fundamental movements of the position.

Coaching Points:

Lead Step: Coach should simulate Power Flow. Be sure LB pushes off back foot in direction of flow and maintains weight on inside half of foot.

Spot Drop and Transition: Coach should then simulate pass. LB opens hips and drops to curl area. LB breaks on arm action given by Coach. LB transitions his feet with very short and limited steps.

Leverage Tackle : LB's feet should become choppy and widen with proper leverage on can.

FRANKLIN & MARSHALL LB DRILLS

Justin Stovall, Linebacker Coach, Franklin & Marshall College

Bench, Pull, Rip Drill:

Drill Directions:

1. LB should press downhill on offensive movement.
2. LB should step, strike with hands, separate, and pull/rip (right/left).
3. The next blocker should wait to fire out until the LB has defeated the previous block.

Coaching Points:

1. LB should not bury head in blocker.
2. LB should strike the chest of blocker with thumbs up, and extend arms to separate.
3. LB should pull/rip to right/left upon extension.
4. LB should remain square and keep pad level down throughout.

Naked Drill:

Drill Directions:

1. Place 2 cones half the length of a tackle box apart.
2. Present run to the LB.
3. Give naked action as QB, roll out, and throw the ball for the LB to intercept.

Coaching Points:

1. LB should plant with his outside foot.
2. LB should open up his inside hip (reverse pivot action).
3. LB should get his head around to look for the middle crossing route.
4. LB should run to get on the hip of the cross route (intercept the ball).

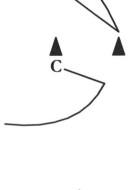

Contain Blitz Drill – (Play to/ Play away):

Drill Directions:

1. Place 2 cones the width of the tackle box apart.
2. Present run action to the blitzing LB's in either direction.
3. Have the QB carry out play-action or naked.
4. Use a ball, and random snap count.

Coaching Points:

1. Both LB's must recognize play to vs. play away.
2. Play to: LB must direct his path to fit the run.
3. Play away: LB must direct his path to the back shoulder of QB.

BLOCK DESTRUCTION
Isaac Collins, Head Coach, Widener University

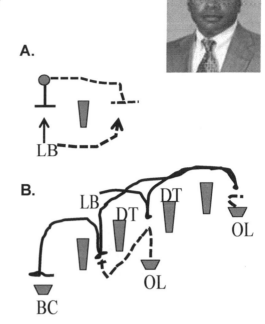

4 Bag Stun:

Objectives:
- Teaching approach
- Teaching hand and feet placement

A.

Procedure: (vs. hand shield or live body)
A. Read OL charge and stun block
B. Shuffle and stun blocker in hole
C. Shuffle and stun puller

B.

Coaching Points:
- Work power steps and shuffle
- Attack power foot with hips open away from BC
- Get hands on target and move feet
- Get off block and Thud tackle BC

4 Bag Down Hill Cut Block:

Objectives:
- Teaching approach
- Teaching hand and feet placement

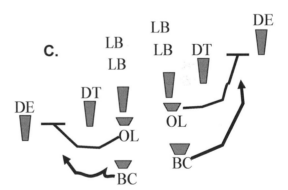

C.

Procedure: (vs. hand shield or live body)
A. Read OL charge and stun cut block
B. Shuffle and stun cut blocker in hole
C. Shuffle and stun puller cut block

Coaching Points:
- Work power steps and shuffle
- Attack power foot with hips open away from BC
- Get hands on target and move feet
- Get eyes on low helmet, defeat block first and then thud tackle BC

LINEBACKER DISENGAGE DRILLS

Matt Hachmann, Defensive Coordinator, Towson University

At Towson University, we will teach our linebackers a multitude of different techniques for getting off blocks. We refer to these as disengage techniques. We will practice at least one of these techniques every day. Because blocking schemes are different, we will use multiple techniques to disengage from different blocks. The following are a few examples of the some of the techniques we use and the drills to help practice them.

Bench/Pull/Rip	**Flow side Rip**
	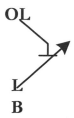
Used on the front side of blocking scheme when blocker presents himself and Linebacker is in phase with the ball and the blocking scheme.	Used on the front side of blocking scheme when uncovered offensive lineman presents himself and Linebacker is in phase with the ball and the blocking scheme. Use against zone scheme.
Align blocker and LB head up 3 yards apart. Blocker comes on 45 degree angle downhill at outside shoulder of LB. LB goes on movement and attacks blocker concentrating on hand placement in the blocker's chest. While keeping a good base, the LB will extend his arms to create separation and then pull the blocker toward him on his backside hip. Once completed he will clear his backside hip with a rip and continue flow side.	Align blocker and LB head up 3 yards apart. Blocker comes on 45 degree angle downhill at outside shoulder of LB. LB goes on movement, presses downhill and rips backside forearm and shoulder through the flow side shoulder of offensive lineman. It is critical that the LB gives resistance as he rips through so he does not get pushed passed the Hole.

Shock & Separate

Used on the front side of blocking scheme when uncovered offensive lineman presents himself and Linebacker is in phase with the ball and the blocking scheme. Use against zone scheme.

Align blocker and LB head up 3 yards apart. Blocker comes on 45 degree angle downhill at outside shoulder of LB. LB goes on movement and attacks blocker concentrating on placement of forehead directly under chin of offensive lineman. Place hands on chest as "shock" takes place. Blocker should be knocked on his heels slightly allowing LB to play off to flow.

LINEBACKER DISENGAGE DRILLS
Matt Hachmann, Defensive Coordinator, Towson University

Up & Under

Used on the back side of blocking scheme when offensive lineman presents himself and the LB is out of phase with the ball and the blocking scheme and is in a defeated position.

Align blocker and LB 3 yards apart with the LB lined up on the backside of blocker in a defeated position. Blocker comes on 45 degree angle and attempts to cut off the LB. LB goes on movement and drives hard at flow side shoulder of offensive lineman. Turn shoulders and head slightly giving impression that you are going to flow over the top. At the point of contact stick flow side foot in ground and replace underneath offensive lineman. Continue to flow to ball.

Club & Hop

Used on the back side of blocking scheme when offensive lineman presents himself and the LB is out of phase with the ball and the blocking scheme and is in a defeated position.

Align blocker and LB 3 yards apart with the LB lined up on the backside of blocker in a defeated position. Blocker comes on 45 degree angle and makes a cut attempt to cut off the LB. LB goes on movement and drives hard at flow side shoulder of offensive lineman. Keep shoulders square. At point of contact, club flow side shoulder with flow side arm and pull backside hip and leg through and past blocker. Remain square and flow to ball.

Skate

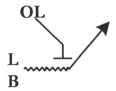

Used on the back side of blocking scheme when offensive lineman presents himself and attempts to cut LB. The LB is out of phase with the ball and the blocking scheme and is in a defeated position.

Align blocker and LB 3 yards apart with the LB lined up on the backside of blocker in a defeated position. Blocker comes on 45 degree angle and attempts to cut the LB. LB goes on movement and reads pad level of offensive lineman. When lineman attempts to cut, place hands on backs of shoulder pads and drive into the ground. Give ground with feet keeping legs free of the cut block. Once block is cleared, continue to flow.

LB DRILLS
Ross Pennypacker, Linebacker Coach, Bucknell University

Mirror Step Drill:

Begin with heels against agility bag in LB stance. 45 degree, downhill read step, reset. 5x, on fifth rep, finish with a burst downhill and come to balance on the cone. Emphasize no false steps or movement.

Block Destruction Progression:

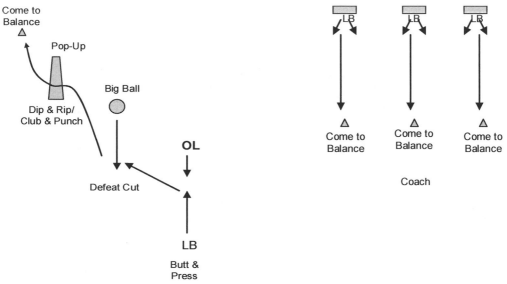

Reaction Drills (always finish w/ come to balance on the cone)

a. Lateral shuffle: emphasize stay square.
b. 45 degree downhill shuffle/tight scrape. Walk tempo.
c. 135 Open, flip hips shuffle, finish with come to balance on coach.

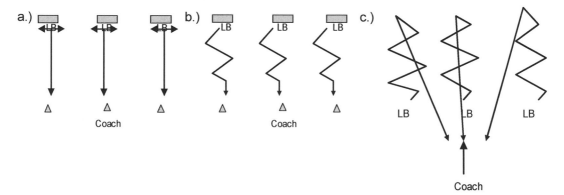

PASS RUSH & BLITZ TECHNIQUE

Scott James, Defensive Coordinator, University of New Haven

Procedure:

a. Set up three cones for alignment purposes. (1) ball / center. (2) offensive tackle or guard. (3) off-set running back. The area should look similar to a ½ line drill.

b. Place a pop-up dummy, popsicle, agility bag, etc. at the position of quarterback.

c. Instruct one of the offensive scout players to "block out" on the rushing linebacker, instruct the other scout player to "block down" on air (represented by the solid/dashed lines).

d. The player in the linebacker position will be rushing off the edge or coming from depth (timing). Give him a consistent cadence or go off a silent count and move your foot. In the diagram the linebacker is depicted as an edge rusher.

e. On your command (sound, movement), the linebacker will attempt to defeat the blocker and finish off with a "high-to-low" tackle on the pop-up dummy (agility bag, another player, etc.).

f. Rotate through from linebacker to running back to offensive line.

Coaching Points:

1. Timing the blitz and hitting a decisive spot on the snap.
2. Emphasizing and maintaining rush responsibility (gap, contain, etc.) based on call / game plan.
3. Rushing with velocity and maintaining aggressiveness regardless of who "blocks out".
4. Emphasize three phases of successful pass rush:
   * Eliminate the space between you and your opponent.
   * Eliminate your opponents ability to block (hand swipe, clubs).
   * Eliminate your opponents ability to recover (clear his hips, reset on QB).
   * Finish.

Variations:

1. Coming from depth versus edge rushing.
2. Use two offensive lineman instead of running back and lineman. Work on protections and maintaining lane integrity.
3. Work in a reach block for edge rushers and teach them to "set the edge" in the run game.
4. Use two linebackers rushing at one time to emphasize "two-in-one gap" blitzes. Have the first linebacker "set the rush" and the second linebacker "read blitz".
5. Use two linebackers on a "rush to cover" drill versus the running back. On a straight line have the lineman set for one linebacker and the running back "check down and out". One linebacker gets rush/blitz work, the other gets man-to-man coverage work.

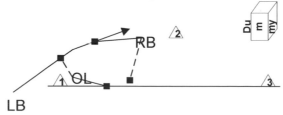

BLITZ REACTION DRILL

Chad Walker, Linebackers Coach, Lafayette College

Purpose:

The purpose of this drill is to teach the edge blitz technique while giving your OLB's game situations to react to.

Coaching Points:

1. RB away widen alignment to blitz flat to front cone (no deeper than 3 yards).
2. RB to keep a tighter alignment blitz path is now the deeper cone.
3. Place agility bags behind the heels of LBs to eliminate any false steps.
4. Teach to "grab the ground" with the front foot.
5. Always finish.

Figure 1: OLB opposite the RB is responsible for Dive (blitz flat) OLB to the RB is responsible for QB (blitz w/depth).
*If you choose to keep the RB in Pistol Formation, teach LBs to keep normal alignment and blitz based off RB's reaction.

Figure 2: Same coaching points as above, now add a naked/boot scheme to have your cutback/naked/reverse OLB react to the QB (good opportunity to talk about angles of pursuit).

Figure 3: Same coaching points as above, now out of man coverage teach your blitz peel technique. We teach our OLB's to peel with the back on a swing route only. If the RB gets up into the line and releases into flat, we continue the pass rush.

Figure 4: Same coaching points as above, now you can coach blitzing off the edge with full slide protection. You can now enter a TE to have them free release or block down with the back filling off the edge. Now we are teaching keeping a contain rush. You can use a dummy or a cut ball to work on using your hands to defeat the cut block by the RB.

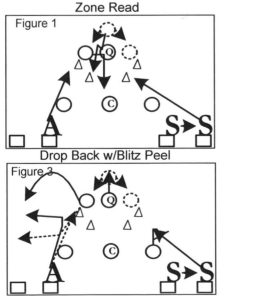

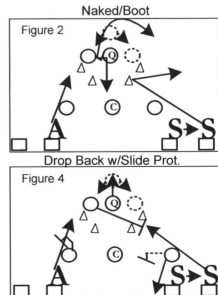

What you need:

Agility Bags or any type of board, Cones or Dots, Shields (if no pads), Football (on stick), Cut Ball or Dummy

STONY BROOK LB DRILLS
Joe Tricario, Linebacker Coach, Stony Brook University

Close Down Drill:

Offensive man backpedals as fast as he can. Defensive man goes on his movement and tries to catch him. Partner is 2.5 yards off of him and should catch him between 5-7 yards.

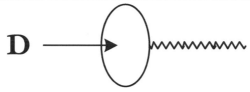

Speed Edge Drill:

Can use cones or partners. On ball movement, defender takes off, executes slap-snake move past first cone or partner. Accelerate to second cone or partner and execute slap-rip, then accelerate to the QB point at 7 yards depth. Be sure to work both sides, time on your movement, and on ball movement. Add turn and sprint through the line. Keep it tight!

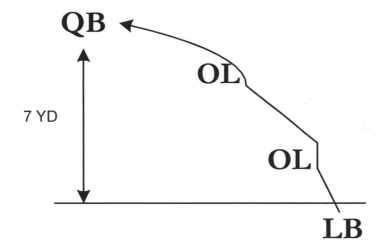

STUN DRILLS

Ron Vanderlinden, Linebacker Coach, Penn State University

Works our backers against the looks they are likely to see in a game
All these drills should last about 8 seconds
All these drills end with a tackle or a turnover

Downhill Stun:

Here we are working downhill versus an outside play. The LB shuffles, then attacks the block with the stun technique. This time the drill finishes with the coach dropping the ball and the LB scooping and scoring.

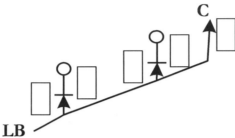

Lateral Change of Direction Stun Drill:

This drill works out and back. The players are numbered in the progression. This time the drill finishes with a form tackle or a mat tackle. PSU often uses hand shields in their tackling for two purposes:

- Saving hits on their players
- Forcing long arms on the tackle

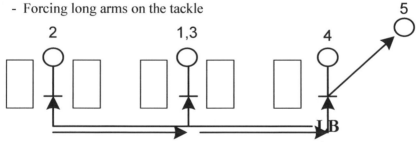

Short Change of Direction Drill:

Like before, we are working our shuffle and stun techniques. Players are ordered in a progression. Coach or DL or extra LB are there to make the drill more realistic as far as negotiating through traffic at the LOS.

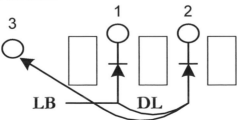

SHOCK, LOCK, & RIP

Randy Bates, Linebackers Coach, Northwestern University

Coaching Points:

1. LB in a good position with his knees bent and hands in a strike position.
2. Shocking the OL with his hands inside of the OL breastplate.
3. Extending his arms to create separation.
4. Ripping through the OL knee to defeat the block.
5. Finish the drill with a tackle or scoop and score.

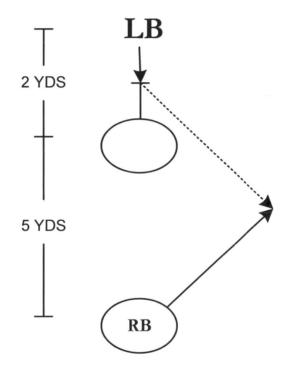

LINEBACKER CUT DRILL

Andrew Poulson, Linebackers Coach, Muhlenberg College

Objective:

To work footwork and contact with hands against cut blocks.

Procedure:

Players shuffle laterally and approach each bag with hands moving and never crossing feet. As each bag is reached, player is to strike front of agility bag with both hands while lifting play-side/cut-side foot. Player is to keep good chopping hand movement and correct posture until end of bag line.

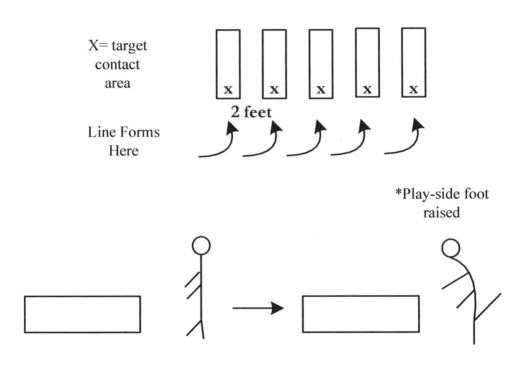

X= target
contact
area

2 feet

Line Forms
Here

*Play-side foot
raised

ZONE PASS DROP FOR LB'S

Mike Toop, Head Football Coach, US Merchant Marine Academy

- Two lines of receivers at 12 yard depth
- LB aligns in normal position with Coach as QB
- Coach drops to pass and LB takes spot drop
- LB reads Coach: see the shoulder and where it points – he also gets his head in a swivel and checks for receivers
- As Coach takes his hand off the ball/goes to throw, LB breaks in the direction the Coach's shoulder is pointing
- As LB breaks, he looks up to receiver trying to get to passing lane
- Coach throws the ball: LB must make Four Choice Decision:
  1. Interception
  2. Knock down
  3. Strip
  4. Tackle
- Ideally, Coach wants to throw ball so LB can make interception

Coaching Points:

1. LB read shoulder while locating potential receivers
2. LB depth on drop should allow him to stay in passing lane

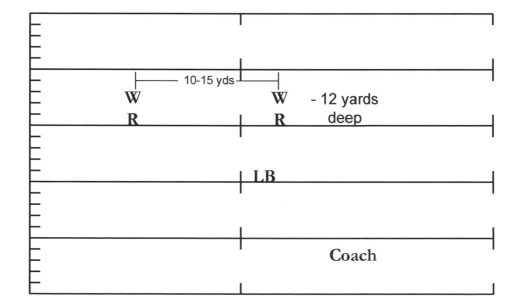

LINEBACKER BLOCKING DRILLS

Tony Kunceweski, Defensive Coordinator, LaGrange College

1. Shed Progression:

   Pair up LBs, each group has a shield

   A. Shed Progression #1
           - LB without the shield is in a 6 point stance
           - On command punch out bringing hips

   B. Shed Progression #2
           - LB without the shield is in a 4 point stance
           - On command punch out
           - Get off from knee, dip and rip

   C. Shed Progression #3
           - LB without the shield is in a 2 point stance
           - On command punch and rip

2. Veer Bag

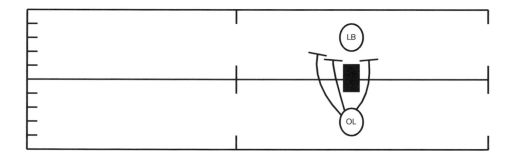

DEFENSIVE BACKS

BITE THE EAR DRILL

Robert Hickson, Assistant Defensive Backs Coach, SUNY Maritime
College

Purpose:

To train the DB to not look back for the football when he is not in dominant position,
stay calm and use the "bite the ear" technique to break up the pass.

Personnel:

All defensive backs. (Can use two cones if needed, 3 yards apart.)

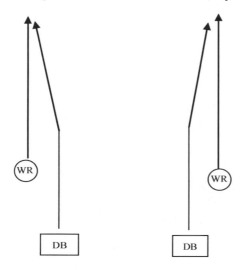

Procedure:

Begin 2-3 yards apart. On first whistle receiver runs a take off route at half speed (holding the
football to his chest). Corners backpedal until second whistle, then turn and run closing with
receiver. Receiver then looks back to receive pass and holds the ball in front. DB must viciously
rake through the WR's hands.

Coaching Point:

Look back only when you are in dominant position (you can see the receiver's front numbers).
DON'T PANIC, make sure the DB rakes through BOTH hands.

Note:

Make sure WR turns with his head FIRST before sticking out the ball. The turning of the head
is the DB's cue. WR should resist the rake.

DOWN FIELD BLOCK DRILL

Joel Quattrone, Defensive Coordinator, Dickenson College

Set Up:

Set up cones to permit reasonable amount of field space to defend. Cones should be placed approximately 3 yards apart so each player can see the boundaries.

Drill:

QB will start play with a pitch to the back. The back must stay within the designated area as he works up field. The defensive back will take a read step followed by attacking the block of the wide receiver. Using different techniques, the defensive back attempts to defeat the stalk block and form up on the ball carrier.

* To keep the defender honest, the QB can drop back and throw the ball to the receiver.

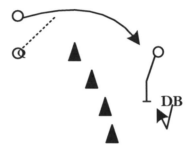

Set Up:

Place one cone in place to simulate the edge of the interior of the offensive set. Place two receivers out in an open set. Secondary are lined up in a Safety and Corner alignment.

Drill:

The QB will initiate play by throwing a flare pass to the RB. As this occurs, the receivers work toward the defensive backs. The safety will attack the block, keeping an inside out leverage position on the ball. The corner will attack his block and maintain an outside in leverage position. The goal of the drill is for the defenders to cut off the running lanes and converge on the ball carrier.

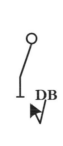

DEFENSIVE BACK TACKLING DRILL USING LEVERAGE AND SUPPORT - CORRECT RUN FITS

Chad Braine, Defensive Coordinator, William Patterson University

This drill works a few things: playing off of the block for the corners, running inside-out for the free safety and the cornerback holding the outside contain.

Set-up:

Need one cone to act as the end man on the line of scrimmage or put a player there.
Need a running back, WR and two defensive backs. We like to do this drill with the wide receivers so they get looks too.

Organization:

The free safeties will line up behind the free safety so they are out of the way and can get ready for their turns right away. The corner backs will align on the sideline ready to jump in right away as well. The WR will form two lines: one behind where the RB is at and the other on the sideline where the blocking WR will be. The wide receivers will rotate lines.

Alignments will be a normal cover-3 or man free look with the corner aligning at 8 yards off. The FS will align 12 yards off the LOS and head-up on the running back.

This drill works on WR stalk blocking, cornerback playing off the block, free safety running the alley inside-out and both the cornerback and free safety working on a good form tackle. We like to keep our players off the ground in the drill and wrap up the ball carrier.

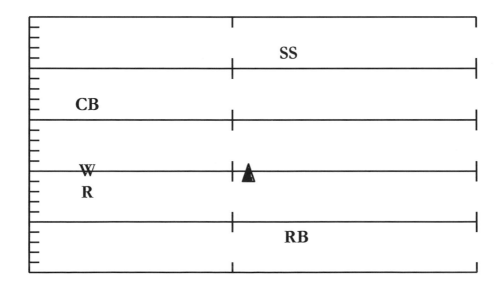

TRANSITION DRILL
Dyran Peake, Defensive Back Coach, University of Massachussetts

Purpose:

To develop the necessary transitional skills required to play defensive back. These skills are broken down into three phases: (1) Pace – transitioning from a slow pedal (read steps) into a fast pedal. (2) Open – transitioning from a back pedal into a full speed run. A DB has to perform two types of turns, Zone (to the QB), and Man (to the WR). Diagram A. illustrates a Zone Turn and Diagram B. illustrates a man turn. (3) Break – transitioning from a full speed run to defend a curl or comeback route.

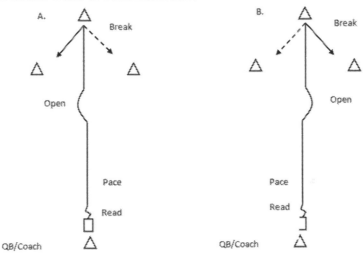

Commands from the QB/Coach: Read (starts the drill), Pace, Open, Break

Coaching Points:

1. **Read** – The DB should "walk out" with his first two steps keying the QB/Coach for 3 step routes.
2. **Pace** – Once 3 step is "cleared" the DB snaps his eyes to the WR and goes into a fast pedal. Once in the fast pedal the DBs feet should "mow the lawn" as he pedals. We do not want the feet coming up to high off the ground. The DB's pedal should "gain ground steady" replacing each step underneath the buttocks, with the arms loose and never working across the body.
3. **Open** – As the WR closes the DBs cushion he must open. When opening, the emphasis is on the torque of the hip and driving the opposite knee over. This should be a 2-step process with the first step coming when the hip torques and the second step coming when the knee drives around. At this point the DB should be in a full forward run position.
4. **Break** – When the WR breaks off his route, the DB must break. The break is a two step process in which the DB stops forward motion with his "break-foot" and redirects with his "drive-foot" by sinking the hips and getting the entire break-foot into the ground, and unlocking the hips by pivoting the drive-foot to the target and pushing of on it. The DB will go where the drive foot takes him! It is very important not to bring the drive foot back or pick it up too high (it should come just off the ground), as this is wasted motion.

IN THE BOX DRILL

Mike Donnelly, Head Football Coach, Muhlenberg College

This is an everyday drill for Defensive Backs. I use this drill at least once a week during the season.

Purpose:
1. To teach Defensive Backs (and even linebackers) stance, start.
2. Teach set recognition.
3. Teach reaction to pass and pass responsibilities.
4. Teach reaction to run (run wheel) and run responsibilities.
5. Teach motion adjustments.
6. Improve stance and start.
7. Improve position specific conditioning.

Procedure:
All DB's (this is critical as there is little rest in this drill that lasts 5 or 10 minutes) align by position, separated by 3 yards, within 10 yards of the coach and the kickers and injured guys, who show the offensive sets.

1. Coach calls out a coverage. All DBs get in the proper stance and the DBs in the front positions make the correct calls. After checking all stances and calls, the coach snaps the ball and moves ball down the line of scrimmage showing run.
2. All DBs take proper read steps, react to the run properly with good technique, yell out their responsibilities in the run wheel, and sprint.
3. After the rep they all hustle back and get ready to go again.
4. Coach calls out the same coverage and shows run the other way or any pass action.
5. Kickers change offensive sets every rep.
6. Rotate players from the front of their lines to the back so all players have to make calls and show they know what to do in each coverage.
7. Add motion after all the basics are covered so players know what to do in each coverage.
8. Run this drill on both hashes and in the middle.
9. Proceed through all coverages. This may take several drills over multiple days.
10. Cover all sets and motions that will be seen in upcoming game.

When individual time gets short, this drill covers a lot of things quickly. You get some agility work, change of direction, stance and start and most important players learn assignment and proper technique vs. opponents' sets and motions.

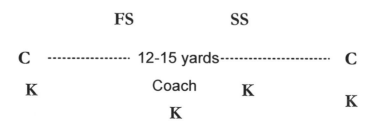

2 ON 1 DEFENSIVE BACK MAN LEVERAGE DRILL

John Loose, Defensive Coordinator, Lafayette College

Drill emphasizes keeping leverage on receiver while working hard to stay square and staying on top as long as possible. Also teaches defensive backs to cut off receiver once receiver has broken cushion.

Drill can be used every day for just a minute or two. Three defensive backs work together. One simulates receiver and the other two line up 7 yards deep and 1 yard on either side of the receiver. Every play, we tell our defensive backs to pick a leverage and keep it. If we have inside help, we tell our DBs to align outside. If we do not have help or are unsure if we have help, we tell our DBs to align inside. By putting a DB on either side of the receiver we are working to keep our leverage from either side.

The drill starts on the receiver's initial movement (Diagram 1). The receiver works hard to get head up and break down the cushion of both defensive backs. He can weave back and forth while working hard to run past the defenders. Both DBs pedal to keep their leverage and keep their cushion as long as they can. Once the receiver gets within 1 to 2 yards of the DB, the DB must execute a man turn to cut off the receiver. The timing of the man turn depends on the speed of the receiver and DB, and the DB's ability to transition. The better the speed and technique, the longer the DB can stay in his pedal. As the DB comes out of the man turn, it is still important to stay on top and keep leverage on the receiver. We work to slap the near arm of the receiver without extending our arm, which almost always draws the flag of the official. Hitting the near hand can break the stride of the receiver, thus slowing him down.

The drill takes about 30 to 35 yards of space and can be done up and down the field in groups of three. You can also take the drill one step further by running actual routes within the bracket created by the two defensive backs. The last step is to add a QB and throw passes into the coverage (Diagram 2). The utilization of this drill emphasizes the importance of defenders to keep their leverage and either use their help or make the QB make the long throw with no inside help.

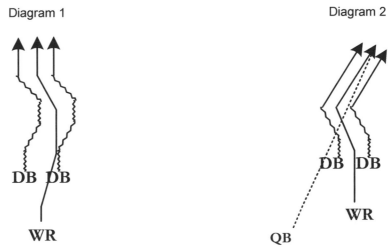

Diagram 1   Diagram 2

W DRILL FOOTWORK & EYES

Jeff Pukszyn, Defensive Coordinator, Moravian College

Being strapped for individual time during practice, I have incorporated three main teaching points into one drill. This will allow my defensive backs to get maximum repetitions in a limited time. The drill is the W Drill.

I will work this drill from the sideline out, moving every 5 yards for a total of 15 yards. The only equipment that is needed for the drill is three footballs. You could also use three tennis balls or soft balls. The three main points that I will stress to my defensive backs during this drill are as follows: One – coming out of the break, Two – eye focus out of the break. Three – extension of the arms when catching the football. Here's how I will work the drill.

The first time through we will do a straight back pedal. On a visual key, the DB will start his break by turning his toe/foot to the outside to make sure he gets all his cleats in the ground. He will then point his opposite foot in the direction he wants to go. I always tell my DB's, you have a plant foot and a directional foot. The DB will always drive off of his plant foot and sprint off his directional foot. As the DB comes out of his break, I will then look at his eye focus. One of the most common mistakes a DB will make out of his break is putting his eyes back on the QB. I want the DB to take three aggressive steps to match the angle of the route before he looks back at the QB. I tell the DBs, if you see the QB throw the ball, you will see the WR catch it! The last part of the drill is getting the DB to be aggressive when catching the ball. He needs to extend his arms and go get it. Remember, the QB isn't intentionally throwing the ball to a defender. The DB will work this for 3 reps down the line covering a total of 15 yards. Each break will be on a 45° angle. Once the first guy in line gets 5 yards, the next guy will start so as the drill progresses we should have three DB's working at the same time. We will then work back to the starting point going in the opposite direction so the DB's work the opposite plant and drive footwork. This will give the DB six reps in a very short amount of time.

Once the first set is completed, I will then put the DBs in a crossover over run for the beginning phase. I will tell the DBs that they have cushion so they can execute an open hip break. The break will again happen on a visual key. As the DB starts his movement, he will plant on his up/lead foot. He will then drive off his directional foot and break downhill 45°. Everything else in terms of eye focus and catching the football is the same as I previously stated. This is a great drill for the DB's when they are in the crossover run phase and need to break on an out/hitch route. Again, this drill will be done going down the line and working back to maximize reps.

The last drill set that I will work is using a crossover run, but now the DB will execute a speed turn out of the break. As the visual key is given the DB will plant his back/trail leg at the top of the break. As the DB puts his plant foot in the ground, I want to see that is head is getting around as fast as possible to make sure his eye focus is on the route and might be back on the QB. All the same coaching points are used in this drill as I mentioned in the previous two drill sets. This will be done down and back so we work both sides of the body.

I will do the W drill at the beginning of an individual period. By setting the drill up as I explained, each DB will be able to work plant and drive, matching the route (eye focus), and ball drills (interception) for a total of 18 reps each in just a few minutes.

DB

Drill #1 Backpedal and Break

Drill #2 Crossover Run and Open Hips

Drill #3 Crossover Run and Speed Turn

DISTRACTION, TACKLE, & STRIP

Joe Nemith III, Co-Defensive Coordinator, Otterbein University

DRILL DESCRIPTION:

Starting on the sideline, a coach and additional player align standing shoulder to shoulder (Coach can even put his arm around the additional player). Align a ball carrier directly behind and between both the coach and additional player so that he is somewhat hidden and the DB cannot see him. The DB should align arm's length distance from the coach and additional player.

On <u>the first whistle,</u> the DB will pedal straight back (stressful) maintaining his pad level (not raising up) pushing for depth. On the <u>second whistle,</u> the ball carrier will accelerate out from behind the coach and additional player to one side and run directly at the bottom of the numbers. Simultaneously on the <u>second whistle,</u> the DB will transition at an angle (inside out leverage), accelerate to the ball carrier, and execute an angle tackle, and strip the football concluding the drill.

I try to emphasis transitioning properly (T-step, or Churning the Feet…whatever you teach), closing the distance between the Defensive Back and the ball carrier as fast as possible, maintaining proper leverage inside/out, angle tackling, running the feet on contact and grabbing cloth to secure the tackle, and stripping the football from the ball carrier at the end.

SKILL WORK:

Stance, Footwork, Visual Cue and Reaction, Angle Tackling, and Stripping the Football.

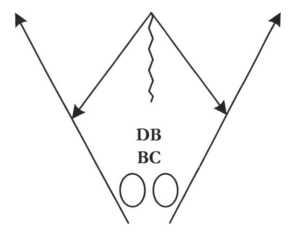

SECONDARY RUN SUPPORT DRILLS

Jeff Mills, Safeties Coach, University of Washington

Ball Level Purpose:

A. To teach the free safety how to read the ball level of the quarterback and effectively execute pass and run responsibility accordingly.
B. To develop a proper deep middle third zone drop by the free safety.
C. To develop a proper fill run support technique by the free safety.

Drill:

The coach aligns a free safety at ten yards directly over the ball and the quarterback. Two pairs of safeties and quarterbacks can be lined up on opposite hash marks. The coach then stands behind the safeties and directs the quarterbacks to move in a certain direction. The coach also gives the quarterback a hand signal of 1, 2, or 3 to indicate at which level he is to move on the snap. The number one tells the quarterback to run down the line of scrimmage. The number two tells the quarterback to drop off the line of scrimmage at a 45 degree angle. The number three tells the quarterback to drop straight back on a five step drop. If the coach gives the QB a number 2 or 3 signal, he will also tell him to either stick the ball out to represent a handoff or he will instruct him to simulate a pass action. The safety backpedals and reacts to a run read by filling to the ball. If he reads pass, he continues to drop to the middle third.

Coaching Points:

The free safety must take read steps. Make the safety yell "Run" on a run read and "Pass" on a pass read. On his fill angle, coach him to attack at an inside-out angle keeping his shoulders square to the line of scrimmage.

Leverage Purpose:

A. To teach proper run/pass recognition on initial read steps by secondary.
B. To teach the force defender to take a constricting force angle vs. run, while meeting and shedding blockers to keep outside leverage on the ball carrier.
C. Increase defender's ability to recognize when primary force has broken down and secondary force is needed.
D. To teach the free safety to take a proper inside out fill angle to the ball.

Drill:

Cones are set up in position of an offensive formation to insure proper alignment of defenders. Remaining defenders are used as offensive personnel. The coach stands behind the defense to observe proper alignment and run support techniques. A one or two finger hand signal is used by the coach to indicate option or sweep. After the strong safety reads run, he will take a constricting force angle to the line of scrimmage vs. option and beyond the LOS versus sweep or arc option. He immediately uses a butt and skate technique to keep the blocker away from his legs. The defender tags or butts off the ball carrier with his inside hand or shoulder to indicate outside leverage has been established. The corner initiates secondary force after the threat of a pass is clearly eliminated. After reading run, the free safety takes a fill angle inside out to the ball and tags or butts off on the ball carrier with his outside arm or shoulder. This is a half-line drill. After the drill is run to the left, the drill is repeated to the right. A second set of offensive and defensive personnel is aligned and ready to go as soon as the first play is concluded to the left.

Coaching Points:

Teach the free safety and corner to play pass first. Incorporate a play action pass to keep the secondary honest.

BACK PEDAL CHUTES
Jack Mrozinski, Safeties Coach, Widener University

Objectives:

- Teach proper stance
- Teach proper takeoff
- Emphasize importance of stance/takeoff
- Keep low pad level

Procedure:

- Check stance
- Check takeoff
- Back pedal staying low under chute

Coaching Points:

- Keep arms pumping and moving
- Keep low pad level
  Can also incorporate all breaks @ 45, 90, 135 and 180 degrees

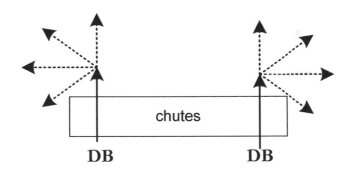

WIDENER CORNERBACK DRILLS

Roosevelt Williams, Cornerbacks Coach, Widener University

Stance and Start:

It all starts here, THESE ARE THE FOUNDATIONS OF A CORNERBACK!

- Feet shoulder width apart with a comfortable stagger
- Start with an "I" not a "V" in your stance
- Bend at the waist, knees and ankles
- Carry your hips high
- Your inside foot should always be up
- Weight on the balls of your feet-primarily on the front foot
- Weight out over the knees, chest over the toes
- Arms hang free, close to body and comfortable
- Hands and fingertips relaxed
- Slight dip in the back, squeeze the shoulder blades
- Chest out, head and eyes up
- Keep knees (when you backpedal) beneath to behind the frame of your upper body
- Execute a smooth and deliberate backpedal
- Your feet should glide over the grass and you should reach the border of your frame with each stride
- Do not get too long in your backpedal, it will make it difficult to make a transition to break on a receiver or ball

4-Cone Drill

Objectives:

- Emphasize importance of acceleration
- Emphasize importance of explosion
- Emphasize importance of quick transitions

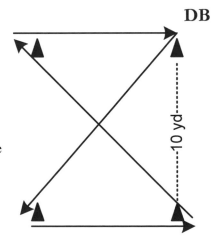

DB

10 yd

Procedure:

1. Boxer shuffle
2. Sprint
3. Boxer shuffle
4. Sprint

1. Angle run
2. Sprint
3. Angle run
4. Sprint

Coaching Points:

- Fluid hips
- Explosion out of each cone
- Accelerate to each cone
- No false steps

CHANGE OF DIRECTION FOOTWORK

Mike Kashurba, Defensive Coordinator, Allegheny College

Open & Break Circuit:

1. Start in square stance facing forward to coach.
2. Open, crossover run or backpedal for depth in straight line to Right or Left (shown) for 5-10 yards. Break on throw.
3. Chop feet or T-Step, accelerate through breaks at predetermined angles: 0°, 45° to the side, 45° opposite, speed turn to opposite side.

Total Breaks:

Open Left, Break at 0° (downhill), 45° Left, 45° Right, speed turn Right (*shown*).
Open Right, Break at 0° (downhill), 45° Right, 45° Left, speed turn Left.

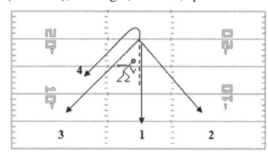

Angle Open & Break Circuit:

1. Start in square stance facing forward to coach.
2. Open, crossover run or backpedal weave for diagonal depth at 45° to Right/Left (shown) for 5-10 yards. Break on throw.
3. Chop feet or T-Step, accelerate through breaks at predetermined angles: 0°, 45°, "Back," speed turn to the opposite side.

Total Breaks:

Open Left, Break at 0° (downhill), 45° Left, back to start, speed turn Right (**shown**).
Open Right, Break at 0° (downhill), 45° Right, back to start, speed turn Left.

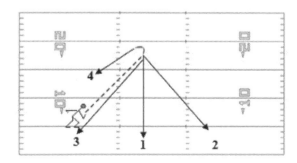

X DRILL

Marvin Clecidor, Cornerbacks Coach, Wagner College

The X-Drill is designed to help Defensive Backs improve footwork and transitioning in and out of their backpedal, as well as improving timing on catching interceptions.

START:

The first DB in line gets in a backpedal stance, while the next DB in line holds up a hand shield/ bag and simulates being a WR.

Step 1. On Coach's command the first DB in line backpedals backwards at 180 degrees.

Step 2. On Coach's second command the DB plants his outside (Left) foot and breaks forward out of his backpedal 45 degrees at full speed to the opposite cone.

Step 3. Once that DB reaches the opposite cone, the Coach gives a third command to have the DB backpedal 180 degrees again.

Step 4. On Coach's fourth command the DB plants his outside (Right) foot and breaks toward the starting cone 45 degrees at full speed.

Step 5. As that DB reaches the start cone, he punches the hand shield/bag with his inside hand and man turns on air to simulate running with a WR on a double move route (Out & Up).

Step 6. Coach throws the DB a high ball and the DB jumps at at his highest point to intercept the football.

Step 7. The DB tucks the ball away and runs it back to the coach. **FINISH.**

The 2nd player in line who was holding the hand shield/ bag becomes the DB and the 3rd player holds the hand shield and simulates the WR. Repeat Steps 1-7 and so on.

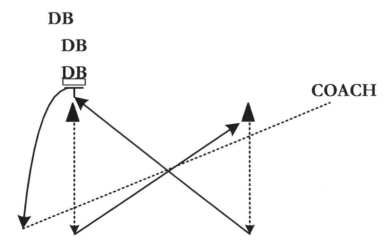

EAGLE DRILL

Meade Clendaniel, Defensive Coordinator, Davidson University

Equipment:

4 cones

Set Up:

Four cones set up in a 5 yard by 5 yard square

#1 – Back Pedal or Side Run
#2 – Speed Turn
#3 – Foot Fire (Drive)
#4 – Zone Drop (Side Run)
#5 – Speed Turn
#6 – Foot Fire (Drive to Coach)
#7 – Catch Ball

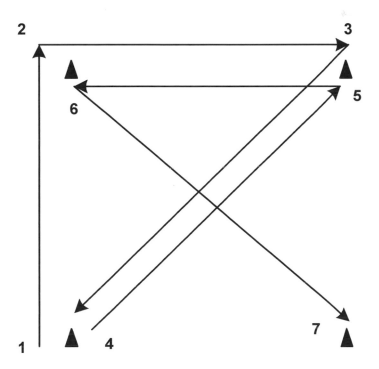

Coach

DEEP BALL REACTION DRILL

David Merritt, Safeties Coach, New York Giants

Purpose:

Training your safeties to back pedal and drive at the proper angles while reading the QB.

Coaching Points:

Low cover 2 back pedal. Stress outside foot plant and drive an imaginary dig for interception. After DB catches the ball have him toss it down. Then drive the post with eyes on coach and speed turn for deep interception.

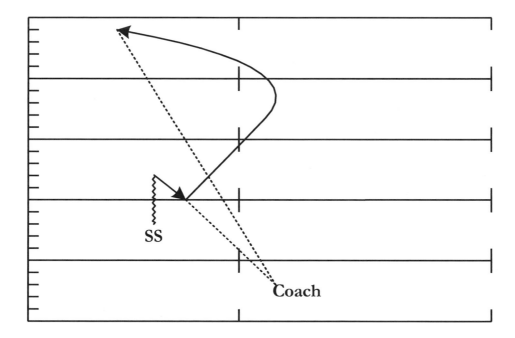

CHASE TACKLING DRILL

Ray Priore, Defensive Coordinator, University of Pennsylvania

Purpose:

Teach open field tackling and stripping for defensive players while also teaching open field running and ball security for ball carriers.

Set Up:

- Use the side line and the base of the numbers as the running lane.
- WR aligns on the 40 yard line. One DB 5 yards behind on stomach, the other DB 7 yards from the WR.
- Coach/QB will say "GO" and throw the ball on a hitch to the WR.
- Chase DB will be on stomach, once the ball is in the air he will get up and chase the WR only trying to strip the ball from behind.
- DB will align 7 yards from the WR. On the "GO" call he will backpedal, then transition once the ball is in the air.

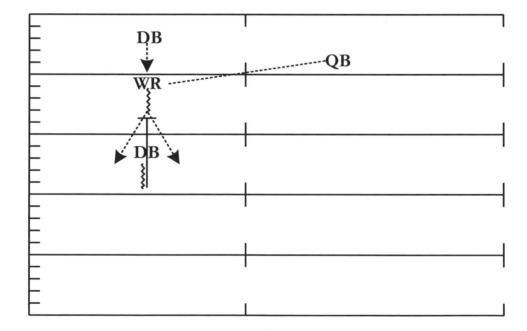

LEVERAGE TACKLING DRILL

Chris Bowers, Secondary Coach, Valparaiso University

PURPOSE:
1. To help players understand how they fit in specific coverages in relation to other positions.
2. To increase the number of "big hits" that comes from players understanding they can run through a ball carrier because they do not have to worry about a 2-way go.

COMMENT:
I initially ran this drill to get different positions working together. We primarily work it out of Cover 2 and Cover 3 pass drops. We saw immediate dividends in the way our defense attacked ball carriers. We emphasized "blowing up" a runners inside leg or outside leg based on leverage. The drill helped them understand where their teammates were, which helped them realize that they were not always in an open-field tackling situation. When they found themselves in a Leverage Tackle situation, we found this drill helped them be violent and attack a runner as opposed to coming to balance like they would in an open-field situation where the runner has a two-way go.

NOTES:
Due to the full speed nature of the drill, we used stand-up dummies to simulate the ball carrier in order not to force actual players to get blown up during the drill.

COVER 2 LEVERAGE TACKLE DRILL:

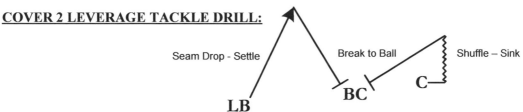

Coaching Points:
- Both the Backer and the Corner should run through the tackle; the Backer blowing up the inside leg of the "ball carrier" and the Corner blowing up the "outside leg" of the ball carrier.
- We usually just use defensive players as the WRs and use them solely for alignment purposes. They do not release. The Corner will shuffle for collision vs. a phantom receiver and sink. Likewise the backer will read Run/Pass and take his zone drop. He will settle, then break on the coaches simulated throw.

COVER 3 LEVERAGE TACKLE DRILL:

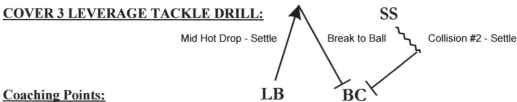

Coaching Points:
- Both the Backer and the Safety should run through the tackle; the Backer blowing up the inside leg of the "ball carrier" and the Safety blowing up the "outside leg" of the ball carrier.
- We usually just use defensive players as the WRs and use them solely for alignment purposes. They do not release. The Safety will drop the way he is coached to in Cover 3 and react accordingly. This can be combined with a re-route drill, but it typically isn't. The Backer will read Run/Pass and take his zone drop. He will settle, then break on the coaches simulated throw.

MARYLAND DRILL

Mark Hendricks, Cornerbacks Coach, James Madison University

I got this drill from Gary Blackney when he was the DC at Maryland, hence the name "Maryland" Drill. I believe it encompasses all the necessary skills of a DB, particularly the transition and break.

The defensive back begins facing the coach. On ball movement, the DB backpedals straight down the line. When the coach points the ball to the cone, the DB will open at a 45° angle and burst to the cone. Once he reaches the cone, he speed turns and bursts to the original line and begins to backpedal again. Make sure the speed turn is as tight as possible. Be sure to emphasize the importance of a sharp speed turn in order to keep it as parallel as possible to the sideline. The coach will then point to either cone and the DB will break downhill at a 45° angle in that direction. The coach delivers the ball and has the DB intercept the ball and give a "Bingo" call.

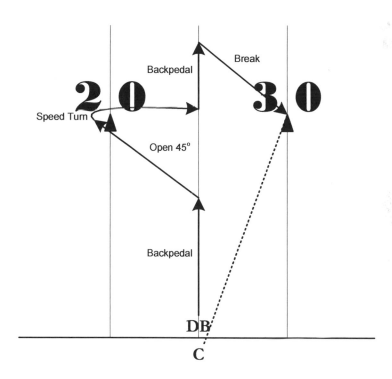

SLIDE-STEP DRILL
Erv Chambliss, Defensive Backs Coach, Union College

This is not a butt weave or cross-over backpedal drill. Emphasis is on staying squared with hips to LOS, mirroring WR direction and movement.

Execute slide step with 3 to 4 yards width at length of 18-20 yards of field from start to finish. Work hard at keeping hips square and staying in proper body position to make an efficient ball break. Remember to work to your right and left equally.

After the initial backpedal the defensive back will engage in boxer-like footwork to the right or left, continuing to get depth then square and break at a 45° angle.

The target cones are at varying widths between 1 to 10 yards from the starting point.

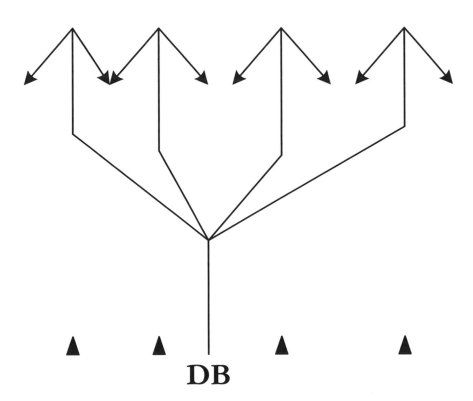

DB TRANSITION DRILLS
Eric Jackson, Defensive Coordinator, Portland State University

One step transition:

This is a muscle memory position. After a lift or winter conditioning, have the athlete stand and do a "one step" transition turn. Ideally, this is done in front a of a mirror to enable the athlete to see if his hips are too high or too low and if the hips are open or closed. It also teaches the DB how important it is to swing the elbows back (to open the hips).

This is also a yoga move. We do it also to strengthen the groin area (this is always an undeveloped area…sports hernia, etc.).

Deep transition:

Teaches players how to run with verticals 25, 30, 35 yards down the field. The example is this: How many times have you seen DBs fall down when covering a vertical or look uncoordinated playing the vertical? This is a way to practice the deep ball and the mechanics of running downfield with receivers.

As the DBs align, the DB playing the WR is pointed downfield. The DB covering has his hips already open and ready to cover. Now it is a race downfield. The DB learns to control his body and tempo.

We always ask the DB to "become a runner" and don't impede the receiver by trying to slap his thigh. Run with your arm over his. A. It looks like natural running motion. B. The emphasis is on running and covering instead of trying to slap a leg. You can give the DB a time count when to look (man/zone turn is coaches preference). i.e., 1001, 1002, 1003, LOOK!!! Just time DEEP BALLS that you have seen. It is usually THREE SECONDS a DB has to cover.

Finally, the BALL is the issue. Let's teach guys to defend the man, then attack the ball.

COVER 2 CORNER JAMS & READS

Corey Wenger, Defensive Coordinator, Lebanon Valley College

Donald Burton, Assistant Secondary Coach, Lebanon Valley College

Set up two cones 4 yards from LOS, with one cone 4 yards from the sideline, and the second cone 9 yards from the sideline (thus 5 yards apart from each other).

On snap, WR will try to run a vertical route inside the cones. The squat CB will jam and funnel the WR into the FS or slide feet as to force the WR to "run the hump" and take a wide path down the sideline.

After the WR clears off the CB jam, the CB's eyes need to find the #2 WR. If the WR is running a vertical stem, the CB will sink underneath #1. If #2 is running an out route, the CB will settle and look to attack the QB's shoulders.

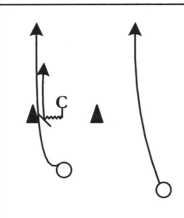

In this example, the CB slides outside to force #1 to run the hump. He then gets his eyes back and sees #2 on a vertical route and continues to sink underneath #1 to provide help for the FS.

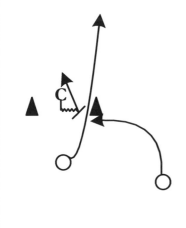

Here the CB funnels #1 inside to the FS, the settles off looking to read QB shoulders for flat attack or to continue to sink.

SAFETY SHOULDER READ

Corey Wenger, Defensive Coordinator, Lebanon Valley
College
Donald Burton, Assistant Secondary Coach, Lebanon Valley
College

- The Safety lines up about 10 yards off the line of scrimmage splitting the two WRs.

- The Safety must read and open to the QB's front shoulder.

- Once the Safety becomes proficient at making the initial read the QB will open one way then
  flip his shoulder back the other way. This flip will force the safety to "baseball"/"speed turn"
  to get back on top of the WR.

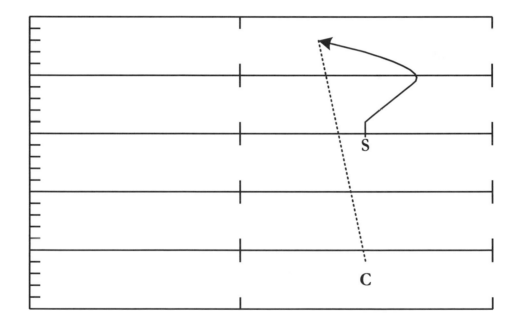

TAKING ON A BLOCK BY A RECEIVER

Bobby James, Defensive Coordinator, Wingate University

There are basically three types of blocks that a DB must defeat vs. a receiver; stalk, cut, and crack. A DB must believe with proper technique a receiver cannot block him!! This type of confidence must be installed in every defensive player, if you're going to play great defense.

Teaching Steps:

1. Stalk Block:

The most effective way to beat any type of block is to avoid it if possible. But, there are many times where the DB doesn't have the opportunity to side step the block and must take it on. If the DB is unable to avoid the stalk block, he must come under control, focusing to the receiver to defeat the block. The DB must be "bent knee" (strike up and through, 45°) taking a power step (outside in – inside leg, inside out – outside leg) as he shoots his hands through the numbers of the wide receiver. The elbow should be in and the thumbs up. The hands should grab the receiver's jersey, elbows locked out (separate), feet continuing to move. The DB's eyes should find the ball as he puts the WR in the running lanes. The DB will throw the receiver as the ball declares. It's important that the DB controls the blocker before throwing and making the tackle.

2. Cut Block:

A. Stay low, be a small target.
B. Get hands on top of the shoulder pads, push off and down, give ground with the feet while bench pressing the receiver into the ground. Use your hat!
C. Focus and defeat the blocker first, and then relocate the ball.

3. Crack Block:

Communications from teammates along with the pre-snap recognition will help the DB play the crack. If the crack can be avoided without vacating run responsibility, do so. If the DB is unable to avoid, attack the receiver right down the middle. The safety must not be too fast across the crack, because the corner is coming down for help force. If the DB that is getting cracked plays too fast across the crack, a seam will open up inside. If the crack is being applied to force, the corner must come down with the receiver yelling crack, assuming force.

TAKING ON A BLOCK BY A RECEIVER
Bobby James, Defensive Coordinator, Wingate University

STALK DRILL

PURPOSE:

To teach the DB to defeat the stalk block.

PROCEDURE:

The DB will be given a coverage. He will drop and then react to the block. The DB must play through the block and not around it.

WR

DB

CUT DRILL

PURPOSE:

To teach the DB to defeat the cut block.

PROCEDURE:

Get a row of DBs on a line on all fours, two yards apart. The first DB in line jumps up and shuffles down the line of scrimmage. The players on their knees and hands will shoot out and try to grab the DBs legs. The DB will defeat the block and shuffle on to the next player until he has gone through the whole line. To get as many reps as possible, the second player in line will wait until the first DB gets through two blockers before he starts. Once finished the DB takes his spot at the end of the line of DBs.

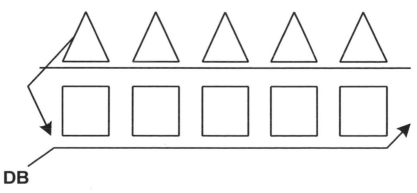

DB

INSIDE, INSIDE-OUTSIDE, OUTSIDE

Mike Rutenberg, Defensive Backs Coach, New Mexico State University

1. Corner & Safety align with base alignment.
2. Coach tosses ball to runner or throw bubble screen.
3. Communication is CB: inside-inside; Safety: outside-outside.
4. CB leverage ball from outside-in; Safety leverage ball from inside-out.
5. Both players must come to balance and close ground to ball carrier.
6. Both players must finish with proper tackling technique.
7. Focus on communication, entry angles, leveraging the defense and tackling.

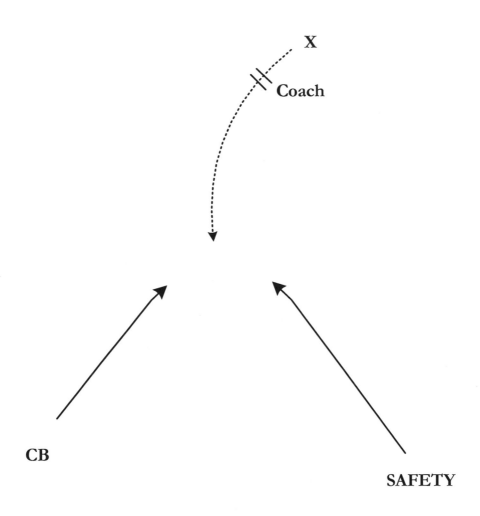

SPECIAL TEAMS

Photo by Michael Garner

SCRAPE PAINT DRILL

Travis Burkett, Special Teams Coordinator, Cornell University

This drill is the difference between a big return for a touchdown and getting a "block in the back" penalty. "Scrape Paint" is the technique that we employ with our return teams to finish plays and ensure that we are blocking through the echo of the whistle without incurring any penalties.

The premise of scraping paint is that our blockers are no longer in an ideal and/or legal position to execute out base fundamental blocking techniques. This most often occurs when an opponent coverage person is faster than us and has beaten us at the point of attack and is now on our returner while we are in a trailing position. The blocker who is attempting to scrape paint must not chase the tackler once he knows he has been beat; instead the scraper must run to the returner and wait for the tackler to close on him. Once the tackler makes his final attempt to close and is close enough to initiate a tackle, the blocker must violently pivot his body so that it is perpendicular to the returner and his front two numbers are facing the returner. While doing this, he must accentuate ripping the arm nearest the tackler so that the blocker scrapes paint off of the tackler's facemask while still avoiding the block in the back or clipping penalty.

What follows is a diagram of how we setup our scrape paint blocking drill. You can setup as many pods as you like – we usually like to have about 5 pods for every 2 coaches. Make sure you get reps going both directions.

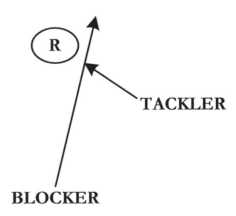

KICKOFF COVER TUBE DRILL

Mickey Rehring, Special Teams Coach, Bowdoin College

This particular drill incorporates multiple phases of the Kick-Off Coverage team; take-off, avoid, break-down, tackle. Have each rep start with 4 athletes located on each sideline and on each hash. The athletes on the hash are there to give a look. The athlete on the far sideline should be equipped with an arm shield since he will be tackled by the coverage man. The coverage man should start on the sideline half way between two yard lines. He must attack the "blocker" located on the first hash. Once the coverage man gets close, the "blocker" will turn and face either direction. At that time, the coverage man should avoid his block to the butt-side and get back into his coverage lane. The same concept is repeated as he approaches the far hash. As the coverage man avoids the second blocker, the ball carrier then runs at an angle to either yard line, forcing the coverage man to break-down, change direction, and form tackle the ball carrier.

Coaching Points:

- Make sure the cover man aggressive attacks the blockers and avoids butt-side.
- Should be done after tackling is taught and practiced since it is a full speed drill/collision.
- The two blockers and ball carriers must be coached up to definitively give a direction to avoid and hold the arm shield tight to the body to decrease risk of injury.
- May be done one tube at a time or all at once.
- Great for practicing KO Cover techniques but also is great for conditioning.
- Cover man must sink his hips when he ball carrier approaches and get his head across the body to ensure a chest tackle.
- May also be done without a tackle phase by placing a coach on the sideline and giving a direction each athlete must finish to.

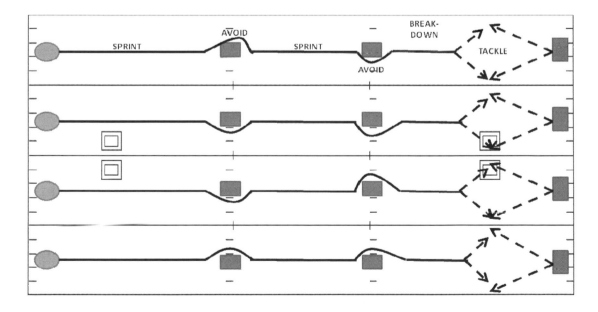

PUNT TEAM DRILL

Bob Ford, Head Coach, University at Albany & Former AFCA President

We have the #1 punt unit on the ball going against our punt look unit. 50 yards downfield is our #2 punt unit and 45 yards downfield is our punt returner.

Our #1 unit comes to the ball and runs 3 plays:
1. Fake Punt – execute blocking assignments.
2. Gunners are live – ball is snapped, the interior 8 block the front, the gunners go downfield against the punt returner.
3. Interior is live – they protect the front and then they release downfield on the punt returner.

At this point our #1 & #2 punt units are together and our look team comes down. The #2 team comes over the ball and executes 1, 2, 3 above. The #1 team then comes over the ball and executes 1, 2, 3.

In a 5 minute block, we have run 3 fakes against 3 fronts, our gunners have gone 3 times vs. anti-gunners and a punt returner, while our interior blocked 3 fronts and covered 3 times.

RET

BACK PEDAL CHUTES

Jack Mrozinski, Safeties Coach, Widener University

Objectives:

- Teach proper stance
- Teach proper takeoff
- Hands "across the table"
- Keep low pad level

Procedure:

- Check stance
- Check takeoff
- Dip and drive
- Run through the block point NOT the punter

Coaching Points:

- Keep low pad level
- Take ball off punters foot – hands "across the table"
- Don't ever give up on the block!

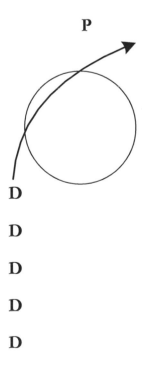

THE WILD BUNCH CIRCUIT

Josh Brown, Special Teams Coordinator, California Polytechnic State University

For us to be great on Wild Bunch (Special Teams) we must be flawless in our technique and our fundamentals. We will accomplish this by practicing fundamentals while providing game like situations. The Wild Bunch circuit has five different stations manned by at least 1 coach at each station. We rotate stations every two minutes to execute all of the fundamentals that are used in all phases of the kicking game. Below are the techniques and fundamentals for each drill.

Station #1: Pride/Lightning Drill (Punt/Punt Return)

GET-OFF:
Once aligned properly and with a clear knowledge of the assignment, the Get Off from the LOS is the crucial first step. Explosion out of the stance, through the proper gap and UP THE FIELD is a must to stretch the blocking scheme. The members of the opposing punt team will view the acceleration up the field as a legitimate attempt to block the punt. The blockers must honor the threat and block with a good deal of intensity. The overall success of this unit is tied to the ability to penetrate with consistent Get Off on the snap.

PRESS:
Once engaged with the proper opponent, use both of your hands to Press on that defender's jersey number, appropriate for the leverage needed, based upon the call. It will be necessary for members of the Lighting Team to become proficient at pressing both sides of the opponent's jersey number. At some point, the force of the initial Get Off and Press will begin to be neutralized by the blocker. At that time after successfully pressing, you will be in great position as you begin to Steel Rod.

STEEL ROD:
As you feel the force of your Get Off and Press being neutralized, open the door, in the proper direction, for the defender to escape the Press. You will then be in position to give the defender pressure on his near shoulder pad. As he is releasing from you, begin to strike with the heel of your hand through the pad of his shoulder. As you are both running down the field, you need to maintain a slightly less than hip to hip relationship, at slightly less than arms length distance apart. As you strike the opponent widen him out of his lane, chase and get back into position to strike again.

RELEASE:
In the other phase of this drill we want to work on best release possible and beat our opponent with speed. Once we have passed our opponent we want to climb back on top so he cannot press us either way.

THE WILD BUNCH CIRCUIT

Josh Brown, Special Teams Coordinator, California Polytechnic State University

Station #2: Strike Drill (Kickoff)

Avoid Opposite:
We will use this technique once we past the 50 yard line and recognize that a front wall blocker is attempting to single block us; this may include a short up-back. In the Avoid Opposite technique we must press the blocker (get as close to him as possible) and avoid away from the side that he is trying to block us. Once we avoid we must get right back in our lane and continue pursuing the ball carrier.

Tackling:
We must be great tacklers on this unit. We will have to execute straight on tackles, angle tackles, and desperation tackles. After avoiding opposite we must begin to breakdown, get back to square and execute an angle tackle.

Station #3: Lightning Drill (Punt Return/Block):

At this station we want to work on our Get-Offs and the footwork fundamentals of the punt block. This drill is performed with a long snapper and punter to get the timing of working proper footwork and running through the block point.

Station #4: Lightning/Regulator Drill (Punt/PAT Block):

At this station we want to work on our Get-Offs and the fundamentals of blocking a kick. This drill is performed with volleyballs to get the timing of turning the corner and proper hand placement while blocking a kick. We want our hands together and our head down…see the ball hit our hands.

Station #5: Wall/Regulator Drill (PAT Block):

This station will be the only station that doesn't rotate. In this station we want to work on defending and getting inside push while getting our hands up. This drill will be performed with a short snapper, holder, kicker, guard, and two defensive tackles. This is a great drill for the interior linemen to get fundamental work.

THE WILD BUNCH CIRCUIT

Josh Brown, Special Teams Coordinator, California Polytechnic State University

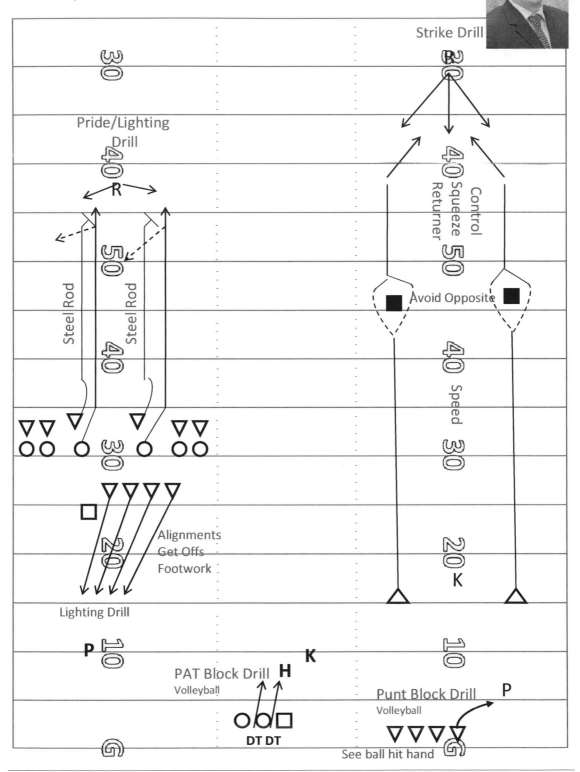

Strike Drill

Pride/Lighting Drill

Control Squeeze Returner

Avoid Opposite

Speed

Steel Rod

Steel Rod

Alignments
Get Offs
Footwork

Lighting Drill

PAT Block Drill
Volleyball

Punt Block Drill
Volleyball

See ball hit hand

DT DT

FUNDAMENTALS FOR COVERING KICKS

Toby Neinas, Linebackers Coach, University of New Mexico

Place a man and a shield on the 30 yard line facing the field.
On the 20 yard line place a second man and shield.
On the 10 yard line place a ball carrier.

Coverage man starts 5 yards away from the first man and shield on the 35 yard line. First shield man turns body on a 45-degree angle to simulate drop and leverage. Coverage man avoids block with a "rip" to the back side of the return man.

Coaching Points:

- Have shield man hold the shield in his front arm allowing coverage man to "rip" the shield.
- Be sure to get back into your coverage lane after avoid/rip of first shield.
- Work into second shield with a good football position and strike with palms into the shield.

Coaching Points:

- Run your feet on contact.
- After shedding the block to the side of the ball carrier, the coverage man executes a good form fit tackle.
- After players run drill, they become the ball carriers. Ball carriers go to shield #2 and then shield #1 to rotate all athletes through the drill. Move up following each coverage attempt.

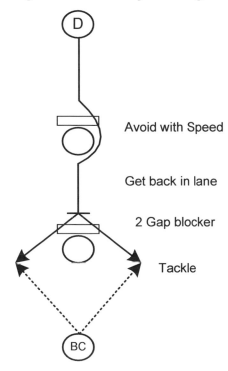

APPENDIX

LAUREN'S FIRST & GOAL MANUAL
CONTRIBUTORS

Coach	College/University	Page
Lew Acquarulo	Trinity College	150 - 151
Dave Archer	Cornell University	71
Nick Bach	East Stroudsburg University	139
Randy Bates	Northwestern University	161
Michael Behr	Moravian College	65
Jeff Behrman	Stony Brook University	63
Bob Benson	Colorado School of Mines	115
Tripp Billingsley	University of Richmond	101
Chris Bowers	Valparaiso University	182
Chad Braine	William Patterson University	168
Scott Brisson	St. Lawrence University	49
Josh Brown	California Polytechnic State	196 - 198
Trey Brown	Muhlenberg College	66 - 67
Greg Bryant	Fort Hayes State University	128 - 129
Travis Burkett	Cornell University	192
Donald Burton	Lebanon Valley College	185 - 186
Luke Bussard	Amherst College	119
Kevin Cahill	University of Maine	93
Michael Canales	University of North Texas	62
Erv Chambliss	Union College	184
Brian Christ	University of Massachusetts	82 - 83
Michael Clark	Lycoming College	35
Stan Clayton	Lafayette College	37
Marvin Clecidor	Wagner College	178
Meade Clendaniel	Davidson University	179
Dave Cohen	Western Michigan University	124
Isaac Collins	Widener University	41, 74 - 75, 153
Ari Confessor	University of Rhode Island	84
Bryan Cook	California Polytechnic State Univ.	64
Ron Crook	Stanford University	18
Kyle Cutnaw	Kenyon College	48
Scot Daap	Moravian College	72 - 73
Paul Darragh	Bloomsburg University	143
Paul Dean	Ohio Northern University	146
Ian Dell	Moraivian College	132 - 133
Jake DerCola	Utica College	80, 88 - 89
Don Dobes	Dartmouth College	112
Tom Doddy	Rowan University	58
Mike Donnelly	Muhlenberg College	170
Joe Dougherty	Lafayette College	136
Charles Eger	Widener University	26 - 27
Kevin Eick	Utica College	40
Mike Faragalli	University of Virginia	55
Mickey Fein	Lafayette College	47
Mark Fetterman	Widener University	131
Curt Fitzpatrick	Utica College	46

LAUREN'S FIRST & GOAL MANUAL
CONTRIBUTORS

LAUREN'S FIRST & GOAL MANUAL
CONTRIBUTORS

Coach	College/University	Page
George Penree	Utica College	22
Paul Petrino	University of Illinois	90 - 91
Brad Potts	Lafayette College	12 - 13
Andrew Poulson	Muhlenberg College	162
Ray Priore	University of Pennsylvania	181
Jeff Pukszyn	Moravian College	172
Joel Quattrone	Dickenson College	167
John Reagan	Rice University	30 - 31
Mark Reardon	Villanova University	120
Mickey Rehring	Bowdoin College	137, 193
Ryan Roeder	Princeton University	95
Bill Roos	Marist College	29
Greg Roskos	SUNY Cortland	59
Mark Ross	College of Misericordia	116
Mike Rutenberg	New Mexico State University	190
Mike Saint Germain	Franklin & Marshall College	138
Erik Scott	William Patterson University	86
Frank Sheehan	Brown University	28
Brian Sheehan	Thomas Moore College	60
Antoine Smith	College of the Holy Cross	130
DeAndre Smith	University of Illinois	70
Chris Sprague	Lock Haven University	148
Dave Steckel	University of Missouri	142
Justin Stovall	Franklin & Marshall College	152
John Strollo	Ball State University	20
Mike Sullivan	New York Giants	57
Joe Susan	Bucknell University	8 - 10
Tony Thompson	Stony Brook University	135
Luke Thompson	Georgetown University	147
Mike Toop	US Merchant Marine Academy	163
Joe Tricario	Stony Brook University	159
Rick Ulrich	University of Pennsylvania	87
Peter Vaas	University of South Florida	61
Ron Vanderlinden	Penn State University	160
Tyson Veidt	Bluffton University	149
Jason Vrable	Syracuse University	78, 98
Chad Walker	Lafayette College	42 - 43, 158
Ed Warriner	University of Notre Dame	23
Tucker Waugh	United State Military Academy	85
Corey Wenger	Lebanon Valley College	186 - 187
Tyrone Wheatley	Syracuse University	78
Brian White	Rose-Hulman Institute of Tech	36
Roosevelt Williams	Widener University	176
Damian Wroblewski	University of Delaware	34
Michael Yurcich	Shippensburg University	56

LAUREN'S FIRST & GOAL FOOTBALL CAMP
VOLUNTEER COACHES 2004 – 2011

Albert, Ben	Blount, Ernie	Cary, Tim	Csencsitz, Dan
Alercio, Rich	Blume, Dan	Casula, Steve	Curtis, Canute
Alt, Darell	Blumette, Sean	Cecchini, Dave	Cutnaw, Kyle
Ambrose, Jared	Bocage, Chris	Chambers, Lee	Czerwien, Mike
Ambrosie, Jeff	Boden, Chris	Cherney, Keith	Daignault, Shaun
Amundson, Bob	Bodnar, Terry	Chesney, Bob	Dakosty, Stan
Andzel, Matt	Borgonzi, Dave	Chimienti, Frank	Daleen, Daryl
Angeleco, Brian	Borich, Matt	Christ, Drew	Damian, Chris
Angeli, Phil	Bostick, Shawn	Christ, Matt	Dan, Blume
Angelichio, Brian	Bowes, John	Churchhill, Jonathan	D'Andraia, Mike
Antonucci, Larry	Boxleitner, Wade	Ciarrocca, Kirk	Dapp, Scott
Archer, David	Boyle, Steve	Cicilioni, Corey	Darragh, Paul
Archer, Terence	Bradley, Curt	Clark, Brian	Darrisaw, Rashid
Argast, Ed	Brady, Collins	Clark, Don	Davanzo, Dan
Arruza, Pedro	Braine, Chadd	Clark, Kevin	Daves, Raleigh
Asselta, Art	Brand, Matt	Clark, Mike	David, Kory
Asselta, Art (Jr)	Brazill, Jim	Claro, Tom	Davis, Jared
Atkin, Tom	Breaux, Darwin	Clayton, Stan	Dawson, Matt
Averill, Duncan	Breiner, Andrew	Clecidor, Marvin	Dawson, Mike
Bach, Nick	Brennan, Pierce	Clendaniel, Meade	Dees, Andrew
Backus, Jared	Brisson, Scott	Coaxum, Tony	Delaney, Pat
Bailey, Carey	Brown, Spencer	Coccaro, Frank	Delgado, James
Bailey, Cory	Brown, Trey	Coen, Liam	Delmonaco, Pat
Ballard, Matt	Bruno, Michael	Coffey, Chuck	DeMeio, Darren
Ballou, Dan	Bullock, Ben	Cogley, Brandon	Dence, Matt
Bandy, Jeremy	Burket, Mike	Coen, Andy	DerCola, Jake
Banks, Adam	Burkett, Travis	Cohen, Andrew	Desai, Sean
Banks, Antonio	Burnham, Patrick	Cohen, Dave	Devanney, Jeff
Baranik, Dan	Burnham, Wally	Coin, Shawn	Devito, Doug
Barbas, Cameron	Burrell, Abbott	Colaprete, Frank	Devlin, Mike
Barbato, Brian	Burton, Don	Colbert, Bret	Dewalt, Sal
Barber, John	Bussard, Luke	Coleman, Kyle	Dickison, Brian
Barger, Kevin	Bussey, Jonathon	Collins, Isaac	Dietzel, Mike
Barnhart, Chad	Butler, Ron	Collins, Mark	Digaetano, Vincent
Barrale, Bill	Byrd, Stephen	Colonna, John	Digiacinto, Drew
Basil, Brad	Cahill, Kevin	Combs, Gordy	DiGravio, Ron
Bassler, Chris	Calcutta, Dave	Commissiong, Jeff	DiLella, Chris
Baumann, Kevin	Calcutta, Nick	Conlin, Joe	DiMuzio, TJ
Beard, Clayton	Callahan, Kevin	Cook, Brian	Dinnocenti, Jeff
Beaudin, David	Cameron, Jeremy	Corby, William	Disch, Colin
Behr, Mike	Canales, Mike	Costello, Mark	Dobbins, Aaron
Behrman, Jeff	Cantor, Charlie	Cowan, Ky	Dobes, Don
Belisle, Todd	Capozzi, Ralph	Cox, Andy	Donaldson, Scott
Berggren, Andrew	Carlin, Brandon	Craig, Chris	Donnelly, Mike
Bernard, Joe	Carlson, Jeff	Craig, Mike	Dottin-Carter,
Bhakta, Satyen	Carnes, Alex	Cramsey, Tim	Dennis
Billingsley, Tripp	Carter, Harry	Crawford, Ryan	Dougherty, Joe
Billington, Kevin	Carter, Josh	Creighton, Marshall	Dougherty, Kevin
Blackwell, Dassin	Carty, Ryan	Crocker, Billy	Doup, Tim
Blanden, Will	Carvin, Jon	Crook, Ron	Dow, Terry

LAUREN'S FIRST & GOAL FOOTBALL CAMP
VOLUNTEER COACHES 2004 – 2011

Downs, Steven	Gallo, Jeff	Harrell, James	John, Dupont
Duda, Steve	Garcia, Eric	Harris, Aaron	Johnson, Derrick
Dudzinski, Keith	Gattuso, Greg	Hatch, Patrick	Johnson, Irik
Duffy, Frank	Gavlick, Bernie	Hatem, Jack	Johnson, Shawn
Duker, Brian	Gendron, John	Hayford, Brett	Jones, Brian
Dunlay, Brad	George, Bill	Haymore, Josh	Jones, Chris
Duppel, Matt	Gerena, Joe	Hazell, Darrell	Jones, David
Durish, Dave	Giacalone, Vinny	Hearn, Ryan	Jordan, Anthony
Durkin, Bill	Giardina, Gabe	Hebron, Ryan	Judge, Mike
Dykeman, David	Gibbons, Jim (Wagner)	Heffner, Bob	Kaleo, John
Edsall, Randy	Gibbons, Jim (CW Post)	Heller, Scott	Kappas, Chris
Edwards, Darin	Gibson, David	Hemphill, Lyle	Karg, Terry
Edwards, Jeramy	Giganteno, Greg	Hendrick, John	Kashurba, Mike
Edwards, Marcus	Gilbride, Kevin	Hendricks, Mark	Keady, John
Eggerling, Rob	Gill, Jonathan	Hescock, Jay	Keating, Tim
Elko, Mike	Gillespie, Travis	Hess, Ryan	Keeny, Dave
Emberton, Kevin	Ginn, Brian	Hetherman, Corey	Keith, Cherney
Eppleman, Bobby	Girolmo, Scott	Hickson, Rob	Kelleher, Mike
Escalante, Alonso	Glenn, John	Higgins, Justin	Kelly, Jason
Evans, John	Godec, Matt	Hobaica, Anthony	Kelly, Kevin
Fabish, Mark	Goebbel, Todd	Hogan, BJ	Kendrick-Holmes,
Faragalli, Mike	Goff, Carlton	Holcomb, Al	Clayton
Farr, Kevin	Goff, Gary	Hollis, Adam	Kenlaw, Jason
Fedick, Greg	Good-Malloy, Nick	Hollway, Rob	Kepple, Tim
Fein, Mickey	Govoni, Leo	Holmes, Clarence	Keys, Rob
Ferguson, Linwood	Govoni, Leo Jr.	Holter, Austin	King, Omar
Ferrante, Mark	Grady, Brian	Horan, Mike	Kingman, Pat
Fields, Nate	Grandie, Charlie	Hostetler, Phil	Klaiman, Marc
Figueiredo, Anthony	Grange, Nick	Houghtaling, Jason	Klatt, Marc
Filbero, Joe	Greco, Duke	Howson, Jon	Kleckler, Phil
Fine, Marty	Greene, Scott	Hoy, Garrett	Klein, Liam
Flanders, Rick	Gregory, Greg	Hoyte, Oliver	Knarr, Jeff
Fleischmann, Dana	Gregory, Ray	Hudson, Keynodo	Knowles, Jim
Fletcher, Albie	Gregory, Tate	Hughes, Hank	Kosciolek, Cazzie
Fleury, Brian	Griffin, Ray	Hughs, Brian	Kosmakos, Gus
Flood, Kyle	Grinch, Alex	Hughs, Roger	Kostelnik, Matt
Florio, Ted	Grinnel, Chuck	Hunt, Dan	Kotulski, Dave
Flynn, Brian	Gritti, Daniel	Iafrate, Mike	Kotwica, Ben
Foley, Ed	Guillerault, Tim	Iezzi, Dennis	Kropf, Tom
Foley, Patrick	Guynes, Jon	Ingram, Ashley	Kunczewski, Tony
Folmar, Drew	Haase, Gary	Ingram, Pierre	Lackner, Rich
Ford, Bob	Hachmann, Matt	Jackson, Eric	LaFontiane, Nick
Foster, Mike	Hafley, Jeff	Jackson, Jonas	Lahew, Chay
Fox, Ben	Hall, Brian	Jackson, Juwan	LaNeve, Tom
Frey, Bob	Hall, Malik	Jackson, William	Langton, Tom
Fries, Andy	Hallahan, Phil	Jakubcin, Branden	Lardi, Marc
Fuller, Paul	Hallett, Mike	James, Angelo	LaRose, Chris
Fumando, Justin	Hamilton, Ryan	James, Bob	Lastowski, James
Fusco, Frank	Hamme, Matt	Jellerson, Kirk	Leavenworth, Chris
Gabriel, Brian	Hanhold, Matt	Jennings, Paul	Lee, Eric
Galarza, Manuel	Harding, Nick	Jeros, Ethan	Lee, James

LAUREN'S FIRST & GOAL FOOTBALL CAMP
VOLUNTEER COACHES 2004 – 2011

Lee, Peter
Lees, Jacob
Leone, CJ
Leone, Matt
LeRose, Garrett
Levinworth, Chris
Likens, Rob
Linquist, Mo
Lintal, Matt
Lippens, Marc
Lippincott, David
Litzenberger, Mike
Livengood, Dave
Livingston, Bill
Lockard, Ken
Lockhart, Bob
Loebig, Niel
Loney, Kevin
Long, Juan
Loose, John
Lorenz, Casey
Loth, Joe
Lotier, Dave
Lowthert, Keith
Lube, Mike
Luca, Will
Ludwig, Eric
Lund, Bill
Lupin, Frank
Lux, Michael
Maciejewski, 'Mac'
Mahaffey, David
Makrinos, Jason
Malloy, Keita
Malone, Doug
Manger, Travis
Mangiero, Jimmy
Mannino, Steve
Mapp, Kevin
Margraff, Jim
Marino, Vinny
Martin, Ben
Martin, Jason
Martinovich, Chad
Massoud, Andrew
Mcardle, Brian
McCarthy, Billy
McCarthy, Ryan
McCord, Bill

McCourt, Mike
McCray, Al
McCree, Mike
McCrone, Ron
McCullough, Jeremy
McDougall, Bo
McEntire, Tom
McFadden, Doug
McFeeley, JP
McGeoghan, Phil
McGorry, Tim
McGuire, Ty
McInerney, Jeff
McIntyre, Gene
McKenzie, Andy
McLaughlin, Jon
Meert, Jim
Mehleisen, Dan
Melnitsky, Mark
Mental, Mickey
Mercado, Richard
Metzler, Kyle
Meyer, Greg
Migliorino, Keith
Militzer, Donnie
Miller, Brian
Miller, Greg
Miller, Tim
Mincey, Damian
Miran, Jason
Mitskas, Joe
Mogridge, Allan
Mohler, Matt
Monica, Raymond
Monos, Jim
Mooney, Todd
Mooney, Todd
Moore, Allan
Moore, Cory
Moore, Ernest
Moore, Randi
Morales, Julian
Morgan, JC
Moriarty, TJ
Morneault, Matt
Morris, Kevin
Morrissey, Andrew
Mosca, Rich
Mosley, Chris

Moten, Mike
Mottola, Bill
Moyer, Jeff
Mrozinski, Jack
Muehling, Mike
Mulbah, Asil
Muqit, Kadir
Murnyack, Mark
Murphy, Lewis
Murphy, Sean
Murray, Dave
Murray, Mark
Nagle, Kiely
Nagy, Rich
Nase, Ryan
NcNulty, Tim
Neal, Jack
Nejman, Steve
Nejmeh, Greg
Nelson, Nate
Nemith, Joe
Newhard, Jim
Nice, Chad
Nichols, Harold
Niemen, Jeff
Ninas, Toby
Nish, Tim
Niumatalolo, Ken
Nolan, Anthony
Nugai, Chris
Nurse, Wess
Nutt, Ryne
Nystom, Drew
O'Brien, Brendan
O'Connor, Matt
O'Connor, Mike
O'Leary, Pat
Opgenorth, Steve
Orr, Garrett
Ostrowsky, Chris
Ouellette, Eric
Overman, Tee
Owens, Drew
Ozolins, Christian
Pace, Ian
Paczkowski, John
Pane, Jason
Pantalone, Vince
Panza, Ray

Parady, Jim
Parsons, Todd
Partridge, Chris
Patenaude, Dave
Patrick, Kevin
Patterson, Custavious
Paul, Dean
Peake, Dyran
Pedone, Mike
Pehrson, Dale
Pennypacker, Ross
Penree, George
Perkovich, Tom
Perry, James
Petitte, Phil
Phelps, Mike
Piascik, Al
Pincince, Chris
Pink, Marzell
Pinto, Dave
Poling, Shawn
Polony, Phil
Potts, Brad
Poulson, Andrew
Powell, Chance
Powers, John
Powers, Sean
Pribble, Stephen
Priore, Chuck
Priore, Ray
Puckhaber, Dan
Pukszyn, Jeff
Purdy, Jordan
Quarterman, Marcel
Quigley, Rob
Rachel, Rich
Rankl, Bob
Raymond, Mark
Reardon, Bo
Reardon, Josh
Reardon, Mark
Rehring, Mickey
Reisert, Cris
Reiss, William
Reno, Ferri
Riede, Dave
Rivera, Stephen
Roark, Mike
Roberts, Donnie

LAUREN'S FIRST & GOAL FOOTBALL CAMP
VOLUNTEER COACHES 2004 – 2011

Robertson, Chris
Roeder, Ryan
Rogosheske, Chad
Rondeau, Andy
Rooney, Jim
Roos, Bill
Rorke, Chris
Roskos, Greg
Ross, Bobby
Ross, Mark
Row, Kahmal
Rumsey, Scott
Russell, Corey
Rutter, Josh
Ryan, RJ
Ryan, Sean
Saint Germain, Mike
Saksa, Mark
Salgado, Jim
Salisbury, Chad
Sanders, Dana
Santella, Mike
Sapp, Chris
Sawyer, Brett
Schaefer, Jim
Schmitt, Jerry
Schmitz, Bill
Schur, Rob
Scott, Erik
Scott, Kelly
Scott, Larry
Sedick, Greg
Sgarlata, Rob
Shaffner, Paul
Shank, Chris
Shaul, Matt
Sheehan, Brian
Sheehan, Frank
Shehl, George
Shelton, John
Sheridan, Bill
Sheridan, Brian
Sherrod, Brad
Shorter, Adam
Shukie, Steve
Shuman, John
Sigler, Greg
Simmonds, Mike

Simmons, Jeff
Simpson, Mike
Simpson, Tim
Sims, Terry
Sinagra, Carl
Sinisgalli, Len
Skalaski, Charlie
Skrosky, Rich
Smesko, Kyle
Smith, Antoine
Smith, Darrius
Smith, Dave
Smith, Kyle
Smith, Robb
Smithley, Chris
Spieler, Marty
Sprague, Chris
St Louis, Patrick
Stanavitch, Rob
Stanley, Ted
Stansfield, Matt
Stevenson, Rubin
Still, Matt
Stovall, Justin
Strollo, John
Strothers, Stephon
Summers, Luke
Susan, Joe
Sutyak, Craig
Svatik, John
Swanstrom, Dan
Szucs, Terry
Tavani, Frank
Taylor, Chris
Taylor, Tom
Thomas, Blair
Thomas, Steven
Thompson, Brent
Thompson, Luke
Thompson, Tony
Tillery, Jason
Tobin, Tim
Tomtishen, Joe
Tracy, Mike
Trainer, Joe
Trask, Ryan
Tresey, Joe
Tressel, Jim
Tricarrio, Joe

Trigonis, Kevin
Troxell, John
Turner, Wes
Ulrich, Rick
Van Zile, Scott
Varner, Josh
Vashel, Steve
Veidt, Tyson
Villapiano, Joe
Vollertson, Jason
Vollono, James
Volpe, JonVon
Bargen, Kurt
Vrable, Jason
Walker, Chad (Bryant)
Walker, Chad (Lafayette)
Wallace, Kevin
Walsh, Alex
Walsh, Steve
Warrens, Jake
Watts, Tom
Waugh, Adam
Waugh, Ethan
Waugh, Tucker
Weaver, Justin
Webb, Kerry
Weber, JB
Wehmeyer, Ryan
Welch, Mike
Welch, Sean
Welo, Carter
Wenger, Corey
Whitcomb, Ron
White, Brian
White, DeMarcus
Wike, Todd
Wilcher, Gerard
Wiley, Clint
Williams, Larry
Williams, Roosevelt
Williams, Shaun
Williams, Tim
Wilson, Larry
Wilson, Rod
Winslow, Mike
Wood, Mike
Woods, Jon
Wright, Apollo
Wright, Brian

Wright, Matt
Wroblewski, Damien
Yannuzzi, Ray
Yarmolovitch, Daryl
Yoder, Scott
Zambrano, Blaise
Zarrilli, Rob
Zataveski, Mark
Zdilla, Larry
Zeiders, Trevor
Ziegler, Dennis
Zweig, Jake
Zyskowski, Michael

Made in the USA
Charleston, SC
19 December 2011